Dylan Frye was born into a relatively rich family of three, his parents and him, but he rarely saw the other two, being raised primarily by a hired nanny. A loner but not friendless, he made it through high school by a thread, spending most of his time forming and controlling small-time semi-legal businesses on the side. After a few months as gofer in a law firm, he decided to marry someone richer than himself and, after his parents died and left him their mini-fortune, he made his way into real estate. He learned, as they say, via street smarts, and slowly turned millions into billions. A few wives and divorces later, and making a foray into gambling, he decided to take a chance at politics. So, without any experience, he ran for the Presidency of the United States of America, and the rest is history.

Novels by David Cope
(Available from Amazon and all good book sellers.)

Novels in the Will Francis Series (computer life mysteries):

    1: Not By Death Alone
    2: Death By Proxy
    3: Mind Over Death
    4: Death Be Thy Name
    5: And Death Comes Searching

Novels in the Doug Cassidy Series (Peru archeological mysteries):

    1: The Death of Karlin Mulrey
    2: In Time for Death
    3: Death at Last

Standalones (mysteries and science fiction [*]):

    Where Thunder Sleeps
    A Winter's Keep
    The One
    Sometime, Somewhere
    The Ballad of Willy Brice
    Thriller
    Cave of the Winding Stair
    Dark Money
    Beyond the Beyond
    To Keep and Bear Arms
    The Last American
    The Renegade Assassin
    The Deep Web
    Take Back Our Country
    Nox Aeterna (Eternal Night)
    Terms of Ascendance

Reviews of many other novels by David Cope

Dark Money
"The best political mystery since All The President's Men." –
Lorna Welsh, The Times.

The One
"A Classic." – Isaac Thompson, Sunday Post.

Cave of The Winding Stair
"A great read!" – Dylan Douglas, The New Times.

Thriller
"An incredible read." – The City Post.

And Death Comes Searching
"A great ending to a wonderful series." – David Somerset, The
Reader's Quarterly.

Death Be Thy Name
"An immensely satisfying novel." – Samuel Basehart, The
California Standard.

The Death of Karlin Mulrey
"Brilliant in every way." – Scott Dyson, Novel Review Quarterly.

Death At Last
"A perfect wrap up of the series." – Conroy Ned, LA Sunday
Book Review.

Not By Death Alone
"A first-class winner." – Donald Salter, The Daily News.

Death By Proxy
"A terrific thriller." – William Bolstrom, Sunday Times.

Take Back Our Country

A Novel

David Cope

TAKE BACK OUR COUNTRY
A Novel

By David Cope

Epoc Books
Printed in the United States of America
© David Cope 2015
All Rights Reserved.
Published 2016.

Acknowledgments

My sincere thanks go to my wife Mary Jane, without whose encouragement and patience this book could never have been completed, and to Larry Prescott and the many others whose advice on the manuscript was extraordinarily helpful. I'd also like to thank the authors whose books helped me find my way in unknown territory. Any mistakes of omission or commission in this book are entirely mine.

Contents

Preface

The form of this book may surprise you, beginning as it does with five different versions of its first chapter, and ending as it does with five different versions of its last chapter. There are reasons for this deviance that I will explain shortly. For the moment, however, think of it this way—you've not only purchased one novel, you've purchased twenty-five novels, with the part between the first chapter and the last being identical. Thus, when you've finished reading the book through one time, having made a random choice of the one to five possible first chapters and the same for the last and not quite liking it, you may choose another version of the first and last chapters, and continue until you've read this book twenty-five *different* times. One reading among those possibilities might change your mind about the novel. Of course, another route would be to put this book down now and never read it. That would be a shame, but the way it goes. Most people, of course, this being a novel, won't read this Preface, won't catch the various versions of the first chapters, and wonder why I've been so prolific in proving the same point five times over. Oh well.

Now for the main reason I've laid the book out in this way. The protagonist of this novel, and he's also the antagonist as well, will sound like an impossible soul, someone that's hard to take and unbelievable. People who run for President of the U.S. cannot be considered this unstable and apparently irresponsible, though many are and have been. Even more so, to be sure, and thus the reason for the multiple chapter ones. No matter which version of the chapter you decide to read, you will encounter a different real life candidate. I've not changed any names. I've not altered the facts in any way. So, by the time you get to the single version of chapter two of this book, you will definitely be prepared for what you'll be facing from then on. My protagonist-antagonist will seem tame in comparison to reality. I hope it won't be a letdown to you as you plow through this character's strange life and how he deals with the world around him. Surely his differences from the opening chapters' real people will keep your attention glued to the page.

In any event, I suggest you randomly choose a chapter one—maybe by tossing a die once and counting its six as a five so only five outcomes are possible—read the number on top after tossing, and immediately choose that version. Reading all five versions of chapter one in a row will not—I repeat *not*—do anything but saturate your brain with unnecessary dogma that will by that time suggest a trip through memory lane on Google under the heading 'nuts running for President.'

When you arrive, which I hope you do, at the final chapter of this book, you should repeat the process described above to randomly provide you with a last chapter. Any of these final five choices provides a slightly—actually more than slightly—final outcome for the protagonist-antagonist, a logical conclusion though with different results.

Before completing this Preface, I will directly address the notion that some might have during or after reading this book that Dylan Frye is in some way a fictional representation of Donald J. Trump, the Republican candidate for President at the time in which I write this and leads in delegates for the GOP convention. This is not the case. Nor is it the case that with any of the five candidates discussed in chapters 1. Dylan is a conglomerate of each of these individuals not a recast of one alone. In fact, more than that, Dylan represents many other individuals who, over the years, decades, and centuries, have taken different routes on their way to winning or losing the Presidential election that they endeavored to win. As this book's first pages state and I repeat here, "The characters and events in this book are fictitious. Any similarity to real persons, living or dead, is coincidental and not intended by the author."

Good luck.

David Cope

1-1. A Reminder

It's often good to remind ourselves that persons of questionable mental capacities have far more than once run for the highest office in our land. Apparently, the words President of the U. S. of A. hold attractions for many, attractions that most of us would avoid at any cost primarily due to the extreme and nearly twenty-four-seven presures on said President to solve insoluable problems, taking the high road whenever possible, and bearing up under the constant criticism of important colleagues, the press, and public no matter how good you think you're doing.

An enormous amount of self-confidence at best and likely arrogance are required to maintain good mental health, and most us don't have such self-important swaggering in their psychologcial makeup. In other words, we are normal beings, not narcissists. Those that do have such imperious and pretentuous thoughts about themselves are generally called unusual at best, like a zebra without stripes, and pathalogical at worst. Thus, an enormous range of usually fifty to sixty or so candidates typically run for the office, most of whom we never hear about because they run independently in parties of dubious origins, or can pay the required fee to be considered a legal candidate. Thus, Presidential elections tend to draw an amazing diversity of the questionably sane to it's count that includes some within the few that make headlines of one sort or another.

As an example, Lyndon LaRouche ran for U.S. President in the most successive elections—eight—once for his own Labor party and seven times on the Democratic Party ticket. In 1992, having been convicted of fraud, LaRouche became only the second person in history to run for President from prison. In 2004, he had more individual contributors to his campaign than any other candidate until John Kerry surpassed him in the final quarter of that primary campaign. He also initiated the so-called LaRouche Movement that promoted his proposal for the colonization of Mars.

LaRouche attended Northeastern University in Boston but left in 1942 later saying that his teachers "lacked the competence to teach me on conditions I was willing to tolerate." As a Quaker, he claimed himself a conscientious objector during WWII and joined the Army in 1944 as a non-combatant serving in India and Burma with medical units. After brief bouts with Marxism and Trotskyism, he joined the Socialist Workers Party adopting the name "Lyn Marcus" for his political work. He moved to New York City in 1953, where he labored as a management consultant and in 1964 joined the Revolutionary Tendency, a faction of the Socialist Workers Party, later being expelled.

For six months, LaRouche worked with American Healyite leader Tim Wohlforth, who once wrote that LaRouche had a "gargantuan ego, and a marvelous ability to place any world happening in a larger context . . . lacking in factual detail and depth." LaRouche briefly joined the rival Spartacist League before announcing his intention to build a new "Fifth International."

In 1971, LaRouche established an Intelligence Network with members from all over the world. This network distributed information worldwide via briefings and other publications using a series of news services and magazines that critics say gained access to government officials under the cover of press passes.

Several local and federal officials stated that they feared security leaks from the government's ties with the movement. According to critics, the supposed behind-the-scenes knowledge was more likely flights of fancy than inside information. Many said the briefings consisted of disinformation, hate-filled material about enemies, phony letters, intimidation, fake newspaper articles, and dirty tricks on campaigns. Opponents were accused of being gay or Nazis, or were linked to murders, which the movement called "psywar techniques."

A 1973 internal FBI letter metioned the Communist Party's efforts to eliminate LaRouche, and cited the submission of a "blind memorandum" to the party's newspaper. Press accounts alleged that between April and September 1973, during what LaRouche called "Operation Mop-Up," his organization physically attacked members of leftist groups that LaRouche now classified as "left-protofascists." Armed with chains, bats, and martial-art nunchuk sticks, members of LaRouche's group assaulted Communist Party, Progressive Labor Party, and Black Power activists on the streets and during meetings.

LaRouche founded the U.S. Labor Party in 1973, at first preaching Marxist revolution, but by 1977 had shifted from left-wing to right-wing views. A two-part article in *The New York Times* around that later time alleged that LaRouche had turned the party into an extreme-right, antisemitic organization, despite the presence of Jewish members. LaRouche denied the charges, and said he had filed a one-hundred million dollar libel suit against the allegations. The *Times* responded by saying that members of LaRouche's group had taken courses in how to use knives and rifles, that a farm in upstate New York had been used for guerrilla training, and that several members had undergone a six-day anti-terrorist training course run by Mitchell WerBell, an arms dealer and former member of the Office of Strategic Services who said he also had ties to the CIA.

LaRouche wrote in 1973 about the use of certain psychological techniques on recruits. In an article called "Beyond Psychoanalysis," he stated that a worker's persona had to be stripped away to arrive at a state he called "little me" from which it would be possible to "rebuild personalities around a new socialist identity." In 1974, through contacts with far right groups and intelligence gathering, LaRouche established contacts with the Ku Klux Klan.

Around this time, LaRouche also worried extensively about so-called assassination plots against him, and told his membership several times a year that he was being targeted for murder, including by the Queen of the United Kingdom, Zionist mobsters, the Council on Foreign Relations, the Justice Department, and the Mossad. He also sued the City of New York in 1974, saying that CIA and British spies had brainwashed his associates into killing him.

In December 1980, LaRouche and his followers started what came to be known as the "October Surprise," namely arguing that in October 1980 Ronald Reagan's campaign staff conspired with the Iranian government during the Iran hostage crisis to delay the release of fifty-two American hostages held in Iran with the aim of helping Reagan win the 1980 Presidential election against Jimmy Carter. The Iranians had agreed with this, according to the theory, in exchange for future weapons sales from the Reagan administration.

To confuse his supposed enemies, LaRouche continued to lob virtual grenades into whatever imagined plots he could drum up. Likewise he continued to confuse those around him. For example, he supported Reagan's Strategic Defense Initiative (SDI), with Dennis King writing that LaRouche had been speculating about space-based weaponry as early as the mid-1970s. LaRouche set up the Fusion Energy Foundation, which held conferences and tried to cultivate scientists with some success. In 1979, FEF representatives attended a Moscow conference on laser fusion. LaRouche promoted related technologies for both military and civilian purposes, calling for a "revolution in machine tools." He later attributed the collapse of the Soviet Union to its refusal to follow his advice to accept Reagan's offer to share the technology.

In October 1986, hundreds of state and federal officials raided LaRouche's offices in Virginia and Massachusetts. A federal grand jury indicted him along with twelve of his associates on credit card fraud and obstruction of justice. The charges stated that LaRouche's group had attempted to defraud people of millions of dollars, including several elderly people, by borrowing money they did not intend to repay. LaRouche disputed the charges, alleging that they were politically motivated.

Eventually, LaRouche's 'heavily fortified' estate was surrounded at which point he warned law-enforcement officials not to arrest him, saying that any attempt to do so would be an attempt to murder him. A spokesman would not rule out the use of violence against the officials in response. While surrounded, LaRouche sent a telegram to President Reagan saying that an attempt to arrest him, "would be an attempt to kill me. I will not submit passively to such an arrest . . . and I will defend myself."

A conviction followed and LaRouche began his jail sentence in 1989, serving at the Federal Medical Center in Rochester, Minnesota. From there he ran for Congress in 1990, but received less than one percent of the vote.

Few remember LaRouche for his escapades, but he lives on in real life and in maintaining many of his contacts. He certainly had moments of lucidity which cannot be discounted, but his methods of fighting first and asking questions later make him one of the best examples of a man gone haywire in pursuit of an unattainable goal, at least for him, in U.S. politics.

1-2. Politician

For many people, the term politician ranks down there with lawyers, which interestingly many in politics also practice as a profession. Often the brunt of jokes with a hint of offensive language present, politicians, unlike lawyers, can but rarely do matriculate from colleges and universities around this land. Instead, they're self-made individuals with fortunes that allow them the luxury of tossing their hats into a ring which they have no real ability to win. A few, however, develop the thick skin necesary to plow ahead and avoid the pitfalls of making fools of themselves, at least in their own minds, and work one side of the aisle or the other for what they can gain from associations with real politicians. One of these, someone who not only stood with the elite of his time but often outranked them in major committees in Congress, was James Strom Thurmond, a politician and magician who survived many campaigns in the Senate, making it no secret that the hightest office in the land stood as his single most important goal.

Strom Thurmond, born in 1902 and dying in 2003 at ninety-nine years of age, served for forty-eight years as a United States Senator from South Carolina. He ran for President in 1948 as a States Rights Democratic Party candidate, and received 2.4% of the popular vote with thirty-nine electoral votes. Thurmond served South Carolina at first as a

Democrat and, after 1964, as a Republican, like many others happy to be a loose cannon and apparently switching allegiances as it pleased him. Controversial during his half-century Senate career, Thurmond switched parties because of his opposition to the 1964 Civil Rights Act.

Disaffection with the liberalism of the national party and his support for the conservatism of the Republican Presidential candidate Senator Barry Goldwater, he left office as the only member of either house of Congress to almost reach the age of one hundred while still in office.

In opposition to the Civil Rights Act of 1957, he conducted the longest filibuster by a lone Senator at twenty four hours and eighteen minutes nonstop. In contrast, in the 1960s he opposed the Civil Rights legislation of 1964 and 1965 to end segregation and simultaneously as he tried to enforce the constitutional rights of African-American citizens, including suffrage. He always insisted he wasn't a racist, but only opposed to excessive federal authority. In 1948, Thurmond stated, "all the laws of Washington and the bayonets of the Army cannot force the Negro into our homes, into our schools, our churches, and our places of recreation and amusement."

Strom Thurmond's first Presidential candidacy came in 1948. The Democratic National Convention took a pro-civil rights stance, angering southern delegates enough that they abandoned the convention and formed their own party, the *States' Rights Democrats*. Strom Thurmond, then governor of South

Carolina and operating under the motto "Segregation Forever," was chosen as their candidate for the presidency against Harry Truman. To say this was an awkward period for American politics would be a serious understatement. Like swearing in church.

He once argued that, "I wanna tell you, ladies and gentlemen, that there's not enough troops in the army to force southern people to break down segregation and admit the 'Nigra' race into our theaters, into our swimming pools, into our homes, and into our churches."

Thurmond continued to support racial segregation throughout his career. He wrote the first version of the Southern Manifesto announcing southern disagreement with the 1954 Supreme Court decision which ruled that public school segregation was unconstitutional.

Confusion reigned in Thurmond's mind concerning this issue that made him somehow a racist while simultaneously a man devoted to ending slavery, though he often raged with himself, even publicly at times.

In 1998, when astronaut John Glenn embarked on the Discovery at age 77, Thurmond, who was Glenn's senior by nineteen years, reportedly sent him a message saying; "I want to go, too." Declining to seek re-election in 2002, he was succeeded by fellow Republican Lindsey Graham.

Despite his failure to win the White House, Thurmond became South Carolina's most notable Senator. He famously compared the abolishing of segregation to the implementing of communism and made many bewilderingly racist comments for which he never apologized, saying they had to be framed in the context of Southern Society at the time.

Six months after Thurmond died in 2003, his mixed-race grown daughter Essie Mae Washington-Williams revealed that Thurmond was indeed her father. Her mother, Carrie Butler, was sixteen years old and working as his family's maid when she became involved with Thurmond, who was twenty-two at the time. Although Thurmond never publicly acknowledged Essie Mae Washington as his offspring, he paid for her education and passed other money to her for some time after. She said that she'd kept silent out of respect for her father and denied that the two had agreed that she would never reveal her connection to Thurmond. His children by his actual marriage eventually acknowledged her as their stepsister. Her name has since been added as one of his children to his memorial in his state's capital.

Strom Thurmond remains today as one of the most notable politicians of the post Civil-War south. He spent his life as a man dedicated to diametrically opposed concepts that he never settled before he died. Maybe his mix-blood daughter could have helped him along a more logical road had he claimed that in fact she was his daughter.

Who knows?

1-3. State of Birth

Birth states and states in which individuals have lived for a long time can bring out the best and the worst in us. People of great conscience and philosophical abilities often demean themselves by breaking into song or reciting memorized poetry when talking about the states in which they live and, contrary to popular belief, associate their states and thus themselves with winning and losing candidates for President of the United States. Or, in cases where great loses have been incurred with such politicians or when dealing with losing candidates that showed during their campaigns a certain lack of, shall we say, class, ignore ever having heard of these people.

Barry Goldwater served five terms as U.S. Senator from Arizona and became the Republican Party's nominee for President in the 1964 election. Goldwater is often credited for sparking the resurgence of the conservative political movement in the 1960s.

Goldwater, the first candidate of Jewish heritage to be nominated for President by a major American party, rejected the legacy of the New Deal, and fought with the conservative coalition against it. He mobilized a large conservative constituency to win the hard-fought Republican primaries.

Rather than shrinking from his critics who accused him of extremism, Goldwater challenged them head-on in his acceptance speech at the 1964 Republican Convention. In words that became famous, he said, "I would remind you that extremism in the defense of liberty is no vice, and let me remind you also that moderation in the pursuit of justice is no virtue."

Goldwater, painted as a dangerous figure by the Johnson campaign in 1964 which countered Goldwater's slogan, "In your heart, you know he's right," with the lines, "In your guts, you know he's nuts," and "In your heart, you know he might." Johnson himself did not mention Goldwater in his own acceptance speech at the 1964 Democratic National Convention.

In a May 1964 speech, Goldwater suggested that nuclear weapons should be treated more like conventional weapons and used in Vietnam, specifically at Dien Bien Phu to defoliate trees. Goldwater charged that Johnson's Vietnam policy was devoid of "goal, course, or purpose," leaving, "only sudden death in the jungles and the slow strangulation of freedom." Goldwater's rhetoric on nuclear war was viewed as quite uncompromising, a view supposedly supported by off-hand comments such as, "Let's lob one into the men's room at the Kremlin." He also advocated that field commanders in Vietnam and Europe should be given the authority to use tactical nuclear weapons—which he called "small conventional nuclear weapons"—without Presidential confirmation.

Goldwater did his best to counter his attackers, criticizing them for their perceived ethical lapses, and stating in a commercial that "we, as a nation, are not far from the kind of moral decay that has brought on the fall of other nations and people . . . I say it's time to put conscience back in government, and by good example, put it back in all walks of American life."

A Democratic campaign advertisement known as Daisy shows a young girl counting daisy petals, from one to ten. Immediately following this scene, a voiceover counts down from ten to one. The child's face is shown as a still photograph followed by images of nuclear explosions and mushroom clouds. The campaign advertisement ends with a plea to vote for Johnson, implying that Goldwater, though not mentioned by name, would provoke a nuclear war.

Ku Klux Klan members supported Goldwater's campaign for the Presidential nomination publicly endorsing him. Goldwater told a news conference that year that, "sometimes I think this country would be better off if we could saw off the Eastern Seaboard and let it float out to sea."

He voted against the censure of Senator Joseph McCarthy in 1954, though he never charged any individual with being a communist/Soviet agent. Goldwater emphasized his strong opposition to the worldwide spread of communism in his 1960 book *The Conscience of a Conservative*, a book that became an important reference text in conservative political circles.

Goldwater's conservative campaign platform ultimately failed to gain the support of the electorate and he lost the 1964 election to incumbent Lyndon B. Johnson by one of the largest landslides in history, bringing down many conservative Republican office-holders with him. The Johnson campaign and other critics painted him as a reactionary, and Goldwater's supporters praised his crusades against the Soviet Union, American labor unions, and the welfare state. His defeat allowed Johnson and the Democrats in Congress to pass the Great Society programs, but the defeat of so many older Republicans that year also cleared the way for a younger generation of American conservatives to mobilize.

When Goldwater returned to the Senate in 1969, he specialized in defense policy. Interestingly, in 1974 as an elder statesman of the party, Goldwater successfully urged President Richard Nixon to resign when evidence of a cover-up in the Watergate Scandal became overwhelming and impeachment imminent. After narrowly winning re-election to the Senate in 1980, he chose not to run for a sixth term in 1986, and was succeeded by fellow Republican John McCain.

In 1975, Goldwater wrote that "The subject of UFOs has interested me for some long time. About ten or twelve years ago I made an effort to find out what was in the building at the Wright-Patterson Air Force Base where the information has been stored that has been collected by the Air Force, and I was understandably denied this request. It is still classified above Top Secret." Goldwater further wrote that there were rumors the evidence would be released, and that he was "just as anxious to see this material as you are, and hope we will not have to wait much longer."

He once said, "I certainly believe in aliens in space. They may not look like us, but I have very strong feelings that they have advanced beyond our mental capabilities . . . I think some very secret government UFO investigations are going on that we don't know about—and probably never will unless the Air Force discloses them."

Between nukes and UFOs, Goldwater possessed the full gamut of a man in the process of blindsiding centrists and attempting to take the nation on a tour of many diverse and complicated trips into Disneyland. The man was not dumb, but had an apparently incurable psychotic and crumbling version of paranoia and hubris.

1-4. Relevance

Since the book you are now reading concerns a man who would be king, in this case meaning President of America, it would be good to know something about a precursor that whould prove relevant to the nature and ultimate destination of its main character.

John George Schmitz, born in 1930, was a Republican member of the United States House of Representatives and also a member of the John Birch Society. In 1972, he was the pick of the American Independent Party, later known as the American Party, for President of the United States.

Schmitz was notable for his extreme right-wing sympathies. By one measure, he was found to be the third most conservative member of Congress between 1937 and 2002, so much so that the ultra-conservative John Birch Society, of which Schmitz was a longtime leader, expelled him for his extremist rhetoric.

In 1982, after it was revealed—and Schmitz admitted—that he had engaged in an extra-marital affair and fathered two children with one of his former college students, his career as a politician effectively ended, as did his wife Mary's career as a conservative political commentator.

Schmitz's views were extremely conservative even by the standards of Orange County. He once joked that he had joined the John Birch Society in order to court the moderate vote in Orange County. Schmitz opposed sex education in public schools and believed citizens should be able to carry loaded guns in their cars. He was also critical of the civil unrest that characterized the mid-1960s. He called the Watts Riots of 1965 "a Communist operation," and a year later sponsored a bill—which failed to pass—to investigate the backgrounds of teachers suspected of Communist affiliations. He also believed that state universities should be sold to private corporations as a curb against student protests.

When Richard Nixon, whose permanent residence at the time was in San Clemente—located in Schmitz's district—first went to China in 1972, Schmitz was asked if he supported Nixon's going to China. He replied, "I didn't care that Nixon went to China, I was only upset that he came back."

In 1981, Schmitz, who was staunchly pro-life, chaired a committee hearing on abortion. Attorney Gloria Allred testified at the hearing in support of the pro-choice position, and afterward sarcastically presented Schmitz with a black leather chastity belt. As a result, Schmitz's committee issued a press release under the headline, "Senator Schmitz and His Committee Survive Attack of the Bulldykes," describing the hearing room as filled with "hard, Jewish and—arguably—female faces." In his apology, Schmitz stated, "I have never considered her— Allred—to be . . . a slick, butch lawyeress." Allred later appeared at a press conference called by Senator Schmitz regarding Mid-East issues, handed Schmitz a box of frogs, and shouted, "A plague on the House of Schmitz!"

Early in 1982, a man by the name of John George Stuckle was treated at an Orange County hospital for an injured penis. A piece of hair was wrapped so tightly around the organ—"in a square knot," according to one doctor—that it was almost severed. The surgery went well and the baby suffered no permanent injury. However, the baby's mother, Carla Stuckle, a 43-year-old Swedish-born immigrant and longtime Republican volunteer, was not allowed to take John George home since some of the attending doctors were convinced the hair had been deliberately tied around his penis. Detectives threatened to arrest Carla and take John George away permanently unless she identified the father. Carla henceforth identified Schmitz as his father.

During a subsequent custody hearing, Schmitz acknowledged fathering John George out of wedlock. He was also the father of Carla's daughter. This admission effectively ended his political career, though he made an unsuccessful run for the 38th Congressional District in 1984.

Schmitz refused custody of the children. Mary Schmitz's close friend, high-profile astrologer and alleged psychic Jeane Dixon whom both President Nixon and Nancy Reagan consulted while they were in the White House, took in the children. When Dixon died in 1997, the children became wards of the state and were cared for by an orphanage.

If someone ever decides to write a book of the craziest things every said to the media, it would have to include some by Schmitz. For example, he once suggested the US could benefit from a military coup to overthrow the government. But in his words, "Not a bad military coup, mind you, but a good one. Like Pinochet's in Chile."

Never a President, but certainly a member of the U.S. House of Representatives, Schmitz exemplified the perfect marriage of extremism, affairs during marriage, and strange views of international relations. Of course, lest we forget, a truely enlarged ego to contrast his son's penis.

1-5. The Run

This is a book of fiction, and as such it represents fictional characters and a fictional plot. Be that as it may, readers should be made aware that what from the second chapter on may seem unlikely at best and irrational at worst, it does not fall far from the truth. Each run for the White House, every four years in fact, involves several candidates that won't make the grade or, in some cases, may make the grade but shouldn't. These borderline candidates encased in reality deserve reflection, and thus it might be good to describe a very real candidate who, in some ways at least, provides an example to give us pause. In this, our modern age, we seek the measure of a person not in the works of their hands, or in the content of their character, but in the videos of their YouTubes. For the sake of sanity, I've restricted this particular candidate for President to those who have registered their candidacy with the Federal Election Commission as an official and legal Presidential candidate. Anyone can register, though it is not required until the candidate raises, or spends, over five thousand dollars. There are no doubt plenty of others who have not reached that bar and have elected not to file with the FEC.

The most surprising conclusion reached when examining what I might charitably call the more "eccentric" candidates is that your average long-shot Presidential hopeful is more likely to be an uncle who owns a body shop up in La Pine and goes to the paperback exchange, than to a Tasmanian Devil Fountain of Dada.

Jack Shepard has long been forgotten by most pundits and those involved with American Political history. He didn't make the big time, and his exploits from afar were a bit over the line compared to most of those reaching beyond their egos for the highest office in the land, or, it may be argued, in the world.

For example, if you think it takes courage to run for President, try running for President and also running from the law, for that's exactly what Jack Shepard did. Thus, his political activities, and there have been many, have been conducted from Rome, Italy thanks to an outstanding warrant for his arrest issued twenty-five years ago after he was accused of arson for burning his own Minneapolis home to the ground.

Shepard is now running in the 2016 Presidential race or at least imagines that he is. Should you doubt his credentials, the following is a quote, including misspellings and poor grammar, from a portion of his website.

"The world we live in presently is so much more dangerous because of stupid President George W. Bush and his unilateral invasion of Iraq and the remove [sic] of Saddam all based on false Intel that the Bush/Cheny [sic] I do not wish to explain all the things I [sic] as your next President must do which is urgently needed to make America a safer place, by immediately strengthen [sic] our military not weaking [sic] it by forcing our best trained soldiers to retire.

"Trump promises American Voters [sic] everything [sic] but he has not explained how he is going to improve the economy and creat [sic] jobs; all he talks about is [sic] he will deport 12,000,000 mostly Latino immigrates [sic] some who have lived in America for over 13 years.

"I will create programs which would give immigrates [sic] without criminal records who can get a job & immediately start paying taxes a path to citizenship if they continue working and paying taxes for over 5 years.

"America is a nation built by immigrates [sic].

"Trump is a heartless rich boy who never had to suffer and watched over 58,000 mostly Minorities [sic] die in Veitnam [sic]; while Trump with 5 deferrents [sic] which Trump lies about, [sic] "I was deferred because I had a high draft number" [sic] he was called up in 1968; the high draft number he recived [sic] was in 1969. Trump did what cowards who don't wish to get drafted do [sic] use their money to get a [sic] expensive Doctor to write a letter so he can be deferred on medical grounds, though on July 9, 1966, his local draft board had scrawled a '1A' beside his name in its handwritten ledger, classifying him as available for unrestricted military service!

"A Republican President will destroy your Legacy; they [sic] have already promised to repel [sic] Obamacare and not honor your Iranian Nuclear Deal, this you know. I even volunteered for the Active Duty in the USAF, and on Feb. 18, 1970 became a Reserve Officer as a First Lieutenant in the USAF; and on July 4, 1970 when on Active Duty with the rank of Captain

a [sic] Sheppard USAF Base at the height of the Tet
Offensive during the Vietnam War; so that makes me
the only Democratic candidate who I [sic] able to
attack Donald 'Draft Dodger' Trump for being a
coward by getting 5 deferment so he would not have
to server [sic] in the United States Military 4 [sic] for
being in school and a 5th for a medical deferment that
he had a doctor write a letter that he had a [sic] could
not serve. But On July 9, 1968, his local draft board
had scrawled a '1A' beside his name in its
handwritten ledger, classifying him as available for
unrestricted military service!

"President Barack Obama would be my
Secretary of State immediate on the first day I take
office!

"To show your support of President Obama as
the next Secretary of State under President Shepard
please [sic] him that you to [sic] also consider Barak
Obama to please urgently and immediately accept my
request!

"Presently most World Leaders agree and work
very well with President Obama. They know that the
only way to achieve Peace in the parts of the world
ravaged by war is through direct dialogue, [sic] if that
miracle would happen and I was elelcted [sic] as the
next President of the United States of America all my
Middle East experiences would give me a massive
advantage over 'Donald 'Draft Dodger' Trump as
President.'

"It is legal to have ex-President Obama serve
100% as my Secreatry [sic] of State; with his
knowledge and 8 years of contacts and friendships

with all the world leaders at this time of war against ISIL only Secretary of State Obama can on his first day at work be up to date on every aspect of our war against ISIL and the Present [*sic*] State [*sic*] of the World immediately. For ex-President Obama to be Secretary of State is legal according to the 22th [*sic*] Amendment and is urgenttly [*sic*] neccessary [*sic*] for the immediate safety and survivial [*sic*] of America!"

Printing verbatim quotes off a website may seem unfair to some, but so is running for President of the U.S. from Italy, at least to a degree. Maybe Mister Shepard's English language skills have waned over the years and not be as sic [*sic*] as they appear here in print. The point is hopefully made with thirty-eight mistakes of spelling and grammar noted, and with others skipped due to kindness on the editor's part. While not explicit in Presidential requirements, one would think that not burning down one's house, not escaping the law by traveling and living in Italy, and having *some* abilities to speak English would be at least implicit in those requirements.

2. Dylan

Dylan Frye, known to his friends as Dyl, grew up in a modest mansion on the East Coast in Delaware with his third floor bedroom high enough to see the Atlantic Ocean crest less than a mile away. Being the only child of two working parents, he knew his nanny better than his father or mother, both attempting to up the family's mini-fortune more than keep the household finances solvent. He attended private schools with average grades, played and fought with his classmates more than studied, and demonstrated a precocious arrogance far higher than his native intelligence would suggest.

More than anything else in his life, Dyl—pronounced like the pickle—wanted love. Not a particular type of love, plain love. To be loved. Those who loved him, he loved back. Or so he said. Truth be known, however, Dylan had no idea what the word 'love' really meant, only that it could bring him what his mother and dad hadn't, acceptance and the feeling that they knew he existed.

His personality proved consistent. Praise those who loved him, and demean those who didn't. A simple and seductive process that made him seek attention and brashly proclaim his simple philosophy to anyone who would listen. Of course, his proclamations would often take the shape of more subtle invitations, but sometimes it was enough to tell people in groups that he loved them and asked if they loved him back. When they did, life was beautiful. When not, it wasn't.

Aside from love, Dyl enjoyed power and money. Distant second and third places, but nonetheless important. Power and money gave the impression of love and sometimes that had to do. Like love, to get power and money required that he have the confidence of those lesser than him in his mind to buy into his schemes so he could acquire their love. It meant creating a pyramid with Dyl at the top and the others at various levels beneath him, and this, of course, meant the world of business and its ability to create power and money, those two leading him and them back to love.

Since he knew from a very young age from watching his parents the rare times he could, power and money often engendered resentment and hate, the opposite of love. Dylan therefore knew the one important thing that apparently his parents did not—the most important word in life: 'acting.' As he exhibited his power, he had to make people believe that he loved them. More importantly, he also had to provide those people avenues that they could use to prove they loved him. He was number one, but also a number one who cherished their love and gave it back, even in bad times when the news often proved disastrous.

This, then, is the story of Dylan Frye, a simple man at the core, but incredibly complex in the manner in which he undertook to manifest and achieve his goals in life. A man whose world became the only world in the universe in which you either belonged or didn't belong, and if you didn't belong, you were lost and without love.

Dylan's love.

3. Memories

Dylan's first memory came from his days as an infant in the arms of his nanny, Anna. She'd fed him from a bottle, he remembered, and could not think of a time in which his mother, his real mother, had fed him from her breasts. Not a big deal, to Dyl at least, but he recounted it to biographers later in life as if it might mean something to them.

His first true remembrance of an actual event came as the result of hurricane remnants that splattered his third-story window with bits of rain and ice and the winds rattling the glass. Scared the bejabbers out of him since storms regularly came from the west and for the most part ignored his side of the house. During the night, this particular storm sounded like someone attempting to break into his room, and he imagined every manner of possible harm that such a person, a big person, could do to him. From there on he required his bedroom door remain open at night so he could call for help from his nanny or parents, if the latter were home.

Kindergarten posed his next great challenge— meeting large groups of people his age, something he'd relish later in life but at this point having spent most of it in his parent's mini-mansion alone he did not. Groups of even three or four frightened him in every sense of the word. Big people, teachers and parents, but mostly small people like him, chattering at one another without reserve with him having nothing to say, mostly because he spent his time crying, but even in those periods when he quieted down he'd had nothing whatsoever to say. To anyone. At any time.

Though he didn't know the word at the time, 'pathetic' described his one and only teacher for the days that turned into months and then years. Sickeningly nice no matter what ridiculous thing any student did. A baby sitter of the worst rank. A simpleton. All she wanted was a quiet room as she watched her flock busy themselves at mostly ridiculous activities. Like having a circus without tents. But little Dyl wanted her to love him anyway, so he did his best to forget his problems and be quieter and nicer than the others. Of course, she pretended to love all of them, but didn't mean it. So he hated her. For a year he hated her. One whole year as he began to grow and develop his latent skills for getting people—the littler people in the room—to love him for real.

He invented a club during recess when the students could talk. Only three members at first, but after that four and five. The primary objective of this club, called the 'manics' for no other reason than that no one including Dyl knew its meaning, with their sole goal to find interesting ways to drive Miss Feinstein crazy without her knowing who did whatever they'd done. Making strange noises outside of her homeroom door after school let out proved a favorite. Make those noises and quietly steal away without being seen. Or maybe outside the lone window in the room. Same thing. Make the sounds, like say of a dying rabbit or something, and run as quietly as possible back to the rest of the group. Or attach double-sided-glue tape to the doorknob of her classroom door before class so her hand would stick to it and be difficult to remove. Best yet, nearly impossible to remove the glue so her hand stuck to everything for the rest of the day. Or at least until lunchtime.

Dyl never found out if Miss Feinstein ever figured out he led the club, if there was a club. Or that the club was behind 'damn,' a word she often used after such things occurred—the mischief they created. He guessed not, though, since she never gave him one of those looks. Everyone talked about those looks she gave those she expected might be responsible. A stare that only the Wicked Witch of the West could match.

In grade school, Dyl's club developed into a kind of fraternity rivaling the Cub Scouts without rules. Instead of rules, Dylan made them up as he went. Those kids he loved were untouchable, those he didn't found life less than pleasant, the latter accumulating Dyl's hate by talking about him behind his back, spreading rumors, attempting to bait him into fights, arguing his superiority which, with his grades, he felt weakened by.

As he grew up, Dyl developed a simple method of giving presentations of his points of view. Don't prepare anything, talk emotionally, and repeat yourself often, look everyone in the eye as if you weren't terrified, smile, thereby affirming your love for them loving you at every opportunity, and, of course, showing no fear, accounting often the victories you've accumulated, and making everything you did a job well done. Lies were never lies, they were points of view. Finally, never apologize. It made one weak in the eyes of those to whom you're speaking.

As the years passed, from grade to grade, Dyl got passing but generally low grades, something hard to figure for his teachers since he was such a nice fellow, generally smart, his accomplishments so prolific, and his friends, so numerous. The type of kid under which in the yearbook everyone would write, 'Most Likely to Succeed.'

But Dyl had trying moments. In sports, for example, he didn't excel. He hated to get his hair mussed, or feared that he might crack or break off one of his teeth. The thought of a scar on his cheek or forehead made him shriek in defiance, so much so that he'd run from the field and lock himself in the shower room. No one teased him, though, since doing so might nix them from the 'fraternity' and put him on the wrong side of the fence that Dyl and only Dyl could do. The top of the pyramid that looked down on everyone else.

By the fourth grade, Dyl had become a force to reckon with, a boy that ran a kind of mob against anyone that dared defy him and paralyze any teacher that picked on him or reacted to his more than occasional wrong answers in class. The punishments grew harsher and more egregious as he himself grew larger and more egregious. Yet, most of the time he seemed so nice, they'd say. Smiling, apparently forgiving his enemies when he spoke of them, and generally asking but one thing of those who followed him so religiously. Love him and he would love you back.

Power and money, while taking a back seat to Dylan's 'mob,' took the form of betting on games of marbles and craps during recess. He didn't play, of course, merely took a slight pittance as he called it from those winning. Like a mini casino, Dyl ensured the games would not be interrupted by the powers that be by giving them the evil eye, something that Miss Feinstein had unwittingly taught him before she resigned to move on to less tension-filled climes. In short, the faculty of the school and the administration had become so intimidated by Dylan, that they agreed to several demands of his that to one from the outside looked like he was in charge instead of them.

Each new grade Dyl entered, he found that his reputation had preceded him. Fifth grade, for example, had several days delay before beginning since faculty at this level had heard of the little beast and refused reassignment to his classroom. Only the beefiest and most aggressive of teachers applied, but it still took several interviews to solve the problem. Interestingly, Dylan had neither muscles nor brawn, but somehow intimidated these faculty as well. Or maybe 'charmed' might be a better word. Little did the administration know that the tax in the 'casinos' had risen and that Dyl had worked a deal where his teachers got shares of bettor's money in lieu of punishing the students for gambling on city property.

Before Sixth Grade, the school's PTA heard about the illegal gang's activities, learning it from their own kids screaming for raises in allowances, borrowing larger and larger sums of money, and selling various items without showing anything in return. From any of it. Somehow, a black hole had opened on the school's playground and their precious children's money was falling into it like quantum gravity had sucked them clean. The parents wanted to know why. Not an unreasonable question.

As this transpired, Dyl showed no signs of anything but love for his 'gang.' The money he'd raised was never spent, but hidden away as was the money his parents apparently made. Into the family fortune it went for some latter day moment when they'd get together as a family and Dyl would know, for the first time in his life, the joy of being a true Frye.

4. The Tribunal

By the end of the first week of sixth grade, Dylan was called before a tribunal consisting of the school's Principle, Vice-Principle, and head of the Parent-Teachers Association, the PTA. Him and them only. Various previous of Dyl's teachers had been invited but refused to show. No doubt they'd witnessed such events before and wanted to spare themselves of enduring yet another display of hubris versus intelligence.

"Dylan Frye?" the Principal's voice boomed throughout the otherwise-than-him-and-them empty classroom.

Dyl decided immediately and instinctively to take the frightened-little-boy approach saying, with a slightly shaking voice, "Yes?" He could immediately see the sorrowful looks on both the VP and PTA representatives' faces. Good choice.

The Principal continued with, "We have reports from several angry parents that you are leading their children, your classmates, in various games of gambling during recess and after school. Is this true?"

"Look," Dyl responded as he'd heard his mother begin talking when he had the opportunity hear her talk, "I'm not responsible for what people say about me, am I? Nor would you be for yourself, would you?" This had the effect of drawing two conclusions from the Principal. First, no one's *responsible* for what others say. He or she may be guilty of something, but responsibility for what others say and being guilty represented two different things. Second, his latter response tossed the ball right back to the Principal to answer the same question he'd asked Dyl to answer. This, of course, produced a likely third problem as in what order should the Principal's response take.

While the man weighed his options, Dyl added, "I will not, in fact cannot, ever apologize for telling the truth." This had the effect of confusing everyone as Dyl had done everything he could not to answer the question, but his 'truth' statement sounded very much like he had. Mostly it made his comments sound like Dyl had been asked to apologize and that he refused to do something that no one had required.

Now everyone but Dyl was confused. The three members of the tribunal looked at one another and agreed by acclimation and only by eye contact, that the Principal should ask his question again. Something that might have happened had Dylan not taken the opportunity to leap into the passing chasm of silence with, "I have great respect for this school and its leaders. You're so smart. Almost too smart for us students. You outwit us at every turn. You say that parents are asking questions and I believe you, I truly believe you because you are so smart. Really smart. No really, and I like that this is so. I really, really like it. You have a lot to be proud of and I'm very happy to be a student here."

The three members of the tribunal looked at one another again, realized that this would only give Dyl an opportunity to continue with his diatribe, and the Principal turned back to Dylan and said, in as clear a voice as he could, "Please answer my question."

Without blinking, Dylan said, "I have, Sir, I have. What would you have me say otherwise? I will not lie."

"No one's suggesting that you lie, Dylan," the Principal said. "I'm asking if you encourage or otherwise engage in your fellow students' gambling."

"Look," Dyl said, beginning again with his Mother's word of choice, "I never gamble and I never lie. Believe me, never. Strangely, I have to say that a lot of people have been asking this question. No, I really mean it. The answer is, I never do it. Never. I mean never. Some people claim that I'm not a nice person. But I am. A nice person, I mean. I've always been a nice person. Believe me, I am."

"Anyone else want to try this," the Principal asked of the tribunal. "Shirley?"

"Do you now or have you ever engaged in taking money from one or more of your fellow students to protect their games of gambling for money from the faculty observing them?" Shirley asked before Dyl could get a word in edgewise.

The room went eerily quiet. No one spoke. No one. A minute passed and another as Dylan stared at the top of the desk in which he sat, not looking up once at his accuser. Without warning, he sat up straight, red-faced and apparently embarrassed, and said, "I can't believe you'd ask me that after what I told you. I never, ever lie. Has anyone ever suggested to you that I lie? One person? One? I'm a likable guy. Really I am. I won't lie. For you or for anyone else.

Now or ever. My conscience is completely clear and that's what I have to say."

Quiet again, but for the slight rustling of crisply ironed clothes worn by the tribunal members as they attempted to figure out how to deal with the clever but still obvious mis-directions that Dylan kept tossing their way.

"Except, of course, for adding that my IQ is one of the highest. But you know that, so please don't feel stupid or insecure, it's not your fault."

The three members of the tribunal glanced at one another, not sure whether to laugh, cry, or call it quits, but Dylan had different ideas.

"I get it now, I do, I really do," he said, to the sincere shock and amazement of his onlookers and listeners. "You think that I'm taking money from my classmates to protect them from you. Right? Am I right?"

In a state of shock, the three elders nodded. Vigorously.

"Well, you can put your minds at ease. I love my classmates and they love me. We get along famously. Absolutely. No really, we do. I stand up for them and them me. I don't have any idea where you got this idea that we don't. We do. I suppose their parents talked to you. Am I right? Well I love them, too. Though they're wrong about me, and wrong about their children as well. Why would I need to protect their children? From who? You? Give me a break. No, really. Give me a frigging break and pardon my French. I would protect them if they needed protecting, but they don't. Hell, many of my best friends are twice as big as me. Why would I need to protect *them*? They should protect me, if I needed them to do that, but I don't. C'mon. Work with me here. Please. Really. And please tell me who I'm supposed to be protecting them from? No really. Who?"

After this soliloquy, the Principal, Vice Principal, and Head of the local PTA looked at one another, completely flummoxed. Dylan had said his piece as well as he could and had done everything asked of him except one. He'd not answered the single question that had been asked of him having to do with gambling. On the issue of protection, he'd merely asked questions of them rather than answering, and for most of those questions, he'd already provided them with their answers. Yet it had sounded so real, so perfect, that no one wanted to break the spell of the moment.

"Now, could I ask you a question?" he asked them, as if he already hadn't. As if their questioning of him had concluded. "Could we extend recess about fifteen minutes? Yes, fifteen minutes. I mean by the time we get out there in the yard, it feels like half our time is already gone. By the time we share the various rides, and I'm including in that working out who's going to ride what and when and you can imagine how difficult that can be. Oh my, what a challenge that is. Let me tell you. By then it's time to return to the classroom. None of us have had a moment to enjoy ourselves. I suppose the teachers here have noticed the fact that we're still as tense as we were when learning so much before they let us out to go there. I know you can see the problem here. No, really. I'm sure you can see it. I ask you this because I'm positive you'll give it the consideration it deserves because you are the kind of people that would do that kind of thing. You are the best. I really mean that. Now can I go? I'd like to get back to class."

All three nodded, vigorously.

So Dylan left the room, whereupon the tribunal let out the unison breath they'd been holding with each wondering what had occurred. They'd met with Dylan and spoken to him for all the good that had done them. Thank God it was over. Yet, to a one, they sort of admired his ability to dance mentally around the room, virtually skirt any issue with which he was uncomfortable though on point at all times, and speak so ineloquently but fluently so as to sound like he was actually making sense. Or something akin to that.

"What happened?" the Principal asked.

"We got flimflammed," the Vice Principal said.

"Boy howdy," the head of the PTA added.

5. Turmoil

It didn't take long for Dylan to sell his business to someone in high school who the 'club' didn't know, and for it to fall from profitable to dead in a week of turmoil that Dyl watched with awe, and learned from. He earned fifty bucks from its sale, but quickly learned that the world of business, at least at his level of operation, had its definite pitfalls. The high-school freshman he sold it to had, apparently, a not so friendly friend who gave Dyl a bloody nose for failing to tell his 'boss' of the manifold problems he'd inherited. Also this friend took back the fifty that Dyl had thought he'd made in the deal.

The bloody nose was one thing, but the taking back of the fifty quite another. From Dylan's point of view, money meant everything—prestige, honor, love, respect, strength, power, and many other attributes he didn't want to relinquish. Thus, getting even, maybe more than that, came immediately to mind. So, without hesitating, he followed the football lineman who'd bloodied his nose and, from his stash of financial cuts from his gambling racket he'd saved, offered the guy twice what he'd been paid to do his number on the guy who'd paid him to bloody Dyl's nose. To get from his boss Dyl's fifty back plus thirty more from the guy to make eighty total, and bring it back to Dylan. The lineman had had his brains socked around so much he could barely add two and two, and thus he took the money, did his dirty deed, and returned to Dylan with the now eighty bucks and a good shake of hands made a bond as he welcomed the high school big shot into Dyl's fold of love.

Getting even felt good. In fact it felt great. Love him and Dyl would love you back. Hate him and Dyl would hate you back. Rather simple when you think about it. Give back what you take. Sounded downright Christian from his point of view. A logical way to run a life that might otherwise become very complicated.

With the grade school administration and the high school guy he'd sold his business to out of the picture, Dylan felt pretty good. Little did he know at age twelve, though, that there's always a bigger fish. Someone out there in the real world that feels the waters like an ever-moving shark can smell blood. Interestingly, this particular shark shared many of the same traits that Dylan had, but more honed and more artfully thought through. This shark was the father of one of Dyl's gamblers, a trained and successful lawyer for one of the largest law firms in Delaware, and someone with enough paid-for free time to give some of it to a millionaire's son if for no other reason than the pure fun of it.

"Dylan?"
"Yeah?"
"Phone call for you."
"Who is it?"
"A Mister Pearson."
"Who's he?"
"Don't know. Want me to ask?"
"No. That's okay. I'll be down in a sec."

Dylan's Nanny left the phone off its hook and placed it face up on the table near the stairs for Dyl when he came down. Following that she went back to preparing dinner for the two of them. Dyl came down those same stairs, grabbed the receiver she'd left for him, and said "Yeah?" into the speaking end of the older version of the cellphones that his parents wouldn't let him near when in the house.

"This Dylan Frye?" said a male voice. An older male voice than Dyl had expected.

"Yes?" he asked, a slightly tenuous waver in his voice.

"I'm Gilbert Pearson's father."

"Gilbert Pearson?"

"Yes. One of your friends at school? Gilbert?"

Dylan tried to place the name but couldn't.

"Do I know a Gilbert Pearson?" he asked the man on the phone.

"You do," the man said.

"Okay."

"You don't remember him? My son?"

"Not right off. No." Dyl was telling the truth. He couldn't remember ever hearing the kid's name.

"He's told me that he knows you. That he belongs to your club."

"Club? What club?"

"He didn't give me a name, but he says you run a kind of club at the school you both attend."

"You mean a club requiring dues?"

"I don't know. Probably."

"Listen. I don't belong to any clubs. I mean I never belong to any clubs. Don't like clubs. Even if I did belong, I wouldn't require dues to be paid. Not in grade school. No way. Did he say that we paid dues, he and I, to this club? Did he say that?"

"No, I . . ."

"Listen, Mister Pearson. That's your name, right. Am I right?"

"Yes."

"Clubs and I don't belong together. You can ask your son. Go ahead, ask him. He'll tell you I'm right. No clubs."

"What about gambling?"

"What *about* gambling?"

"He says he and his friends have to pay you to keep the teachers from breaking up their games."

"What kind of games? Gambling you say. You mean like gambling on the weather? That it doesn't rain on a particular day. Or games like craps where you play for money based on chance?"

"Yes, like craps. Like they play in casinos?"

"In Las Vegas and New Jersey and on Indian Reservations?"

"Yeah, like those."

"He says he plays craps in casinos? At school? Mister Pearson, I think you should get Gilbert. That his name?"

"Yes."

"I think you should get Gilbert some help if he's going off to casinos in other states to gamble. I mean he needs some real help. Oh my God, I can't believe it. No wonder I don't know the kid. He's driving to strange places and gambling there."

"No, he's not. He's gambling at your school and claims you're taking a cut to protect them."

"Them? Who's them?"

"The other kids in the club."

"The club, again. What's with the club, anyway? I don't belong to any clubs, especially a casino club."

"It's not a casino, it's a group of kids that play craps together at the same school that you attend."

"Right. I see what you're saying. So you think I'm lying, huh. Well, Mister Pearson, I don't ever lie. You can ask those kids if I lie. You can ask your son if I lie. I don't. No really, I don't lie. I truly don't. Anyone can tell you that. I don't lie. As for gambling, I don't do that either. I've heard of craps, but don't know how the game's played. Honestly. You can trust me as I've proved before. Believe me, I would never, ever lie about anything. Do you believe me? About lying, I mean."

"I don't know."

"You don't know? Well ask around. You'll find out. I do not ever lie. Really. It's a kind of thing with me. Always tell the truth. Always. Listen, you can truly count on me against lying. Only gets you into trouble. That's the truth of it."

"I see."

"I hope you do, Mister Pearson. I hope you do. For it's the truth. Did you know that?"

"I do now."

"Good. So, have I answered your questions?"

"No."

"Which one did I miss?"

"Do you take a cut of the winner's take in my son's gambling at recess in school?"

"That was very well put, Mister Pearson. I mean, very, very well put. Succinct as my nanny would say. Right to the point. Listen, and I kid you not about this, I had a meeting with some school authorities about such a thing within the last week. They found me innocent. But, I tell you, and this is the truth, no really. Some kid, some bully hired someone from high school to come and beat me up. He almost broke my nose. All for nothing. Right? For nothing. So here I am, telling you the truth which I am, and telling the school the truth, and what you give me is nothing but more questions about what I did and a goon beating me up. Now how fair is that? I told you the truth. It's not that I don't respect you, but you can see where it's getting a bit old here. Right? Look, if you want to know the answer to your question, ask your kid, Gilbert what's his name. If he tells you his problem is me, don't believe him. You know after we're talking here that I'm not lying and I've told you everything I know, so it must be him lying. Maybe someone at school is threatening him and making me the scapegoat. No, really. The scapegoat. Me, of all people. Now that we're such good friends I'm sure you wouldn't want me to get in trouble. Me, the one who was clobbered by a bully for no reason, right? And cleared by the Principal, the Vice Principal, and the head of the PTA for God's sake."

"Dylan?"

"Yes."

"Go to law school."

"Huh?"

"You'll go far, let me tell you. No, really."

He hung up.

6. Makeover

In high school, Dylan began his most successful ventures yet, the most aggressive being a restoration outfit consisting of school dropouts who purchased suspect used objects from garage sales and the like, painted and gave them makeovers so they appeared new, and sold them for many times the price they'd paid for them. A simple process that took place in Dyl's otherwise unused multi-car garage and run by him from a utility room that he used for an office. As with the take he'd made from his casino-less gambling operation, he didn't need the cut he collected from sales, but took it anyway, bankrolled it, and the business gave him the experience he thought he needed to make it big time in the real world of business.

The only thing illegal about his operations was his lack of a proper license and therefore the paying of taxes. 'Under the radar' he called it, and the minute he felt a slight pressure from the powers that be, he closed down his operations and focused on another that had not yet been discovered. Thus, while he did just enough studying to keep from getting tossed out of high school, he shuffled his various businesses to make quite a substantial amount of money, store it away in his bedroom ceiling, and learn the valuable lessons that *life* taught him, not teachers.

His biggest successes came from brokering deals between two young people from rich families who didn't know one another and trying to unload something they didn't want. Take 'Joe,' for example, who'd harassed his rich parents into buying him a motor scooter for his birthday and who had now become old enough to own a Harley. Take 'Bill,' for example, who talked his parents into buying him a professional drum kit for his career in rock music, but realized he couldn't make the grade and wanted a guitar instead. Neither wanted what the other needed to sell until they met Dylan. His job, Dyl's job that is, was to convince Joe he needed a drum kit and Bill he needed a motor scooter. Brokering meant that Dyl had to seal the deal with a slight cut from the sales prices.

"Listen," Dyl would begin, say with Joe, "you want a Harley, right? Am I right?"

"Yeah," Joe would say.

"Well, you gotta understand that no one's going to give you a Harley for your scooter, see?"

"Right."

"But they might for a really classy drum kit."

"You mean, I trade for the drum kit, sell it to the guy with the Harley, and I'm a happy dude?"

"Took the words right outta my mouth, Joe. Right out of my mouth. No, I mean it. Right outta my mouth. I mean, who doesn't want a first-class professional-grade drum kit? Everyone does."

"I guess so," Joe would say, and Dyl had made at least a cut from both Joe and Bill and sometimes from the next sales as well. From his perspective, this often meant hundreds of dollars after only spending a half hour or so on the job, and, since Joe didn't know Bill, had never heard of him, issues of who did what to whom after the fact never amounted to much of anything. No bullies coming to beat the crap out of Dyl.

All that changed, however, when Dylan decided to accept a deal from two rival gangs to act as a mediator to bring peace to the streets by developing boundaries between the two groups. Dylan's groups, and by now he had many ever-changing such groups, advised him to stay out of it.

"Why?" he asked them. "Listen, making peace isn't hard if you know how to do it." Of course, like most things in Dyl's mind by this time, he could do it, if no one else could. "This is my favorite thing, no, it really is," he'd say. "We'll get 'em together and show them that it's in their best interests to call off the violence against one another and aim it at the cops. Right? The cops are their real enemy, not each other. Only makes sense, right?"

So Dylan brought the two gangs together in the same room and before he could say a word to them, they said the words, and the place broke out in pure violence and hatred, sending several to the hospital and Dyl into retreat. He spent the next week nursing cuts on his arms and face and attempting to get the owner of the warehouse in which they'd met to call off his lawyers expecting Dylan to pay for damages, he being the only one not a member of either gang present that evening.

Ever hopeful, Dylan met with the gangs separately, this time, telling both sides much the same thing. "Listen. I love you guys. You know that. I understand your point of view on this thing. I really do. But war between gangs is self-destructive. You're the losers as well as them. I mean that, I really do. Look at you. Look at them. I mean, *look* at them. I admit they started it. Dumb asses. They don't belong on the same streets as you do. They're the problem group, not us. I mean that. I really do. It's unbelievable. Really unbelievable. They started it and they don't belong. Right? I mean, am I right? So let's do ourselves a favor, shall we. A favor? Let me handle this. You guys, the good guys, lay out a plan for how you'd like the city here to look on paper. How you want it to look. Don't hold back. Tell me what you want. *Actually want*, and I'll take it to them and get a deal. Okay? Is that right? I'll get you exactly what you want and things will get back to normal. Everyone will be happy, right? Am I right? Sure."

Patented Dyl, some might say, and both sides, independently, told him 'sure.' Of course, the two plans proved completely ridiculous and impossible to reconcile. At least on paper. Dyl could see that, but the two groups could not since he never shared the plans with the opposing groups. In fact, he tore them up without telling them and instead told each group that things looked promising and that he was working out the minor details and to keep the faith. Things as important as this took time. He was on it, and the truth will out. In the meantime, though, he suggested that both groups maintain a neutral zone as an act of faith that this would soon pass. A strip of neutrality down through the center of the city in which both sides promised to keep out. Thus, the ceasefire, as he called it, would be the act of trust that both sides kept to prove they would follow the eventual plan to the letter once he got the details ironed out so each side would be happy.

By this time, unfortunately, Dyl realized that his initial plan—to never provide anyone with any kind of a revised final solution—would never come to fruition, and he grew despondent. Yes, he was sure that both sides would tire of the ceasefire zone and ultimately demand some results from Dylan putting him in danger that he could put off for only so long. Yes, they wouldn't pay him anything for the most of nothing he'd provide them. Yes, he'd put his family, his nanny, the mini-mansion he still lived in, and his parents at odds with two groups of pathological insane members. This, then, became a burning fuse that would eventually detonate in his hands if he didn't do something about it first.

So, Dylan did the only thing he could given the circumstances. He met with both groups separately and told them that the other side had broken their promises to him and to them regarding everything. No agreement, breaking the demilitarized zone, and lying about what they said they'd do. After that, he went home and buried himself under the covers of his bed and listened as the sirens roared and the city burned and things returned to its status before he'd intervened. Except now, people were being hospitalized, murdered, and vandalized like never before.

But Dylan was safe, at least for the moment. Until someone told another someone that he'd lied to both sides, which if it occurred, would force him to leave town and make his way by himself. As luck would have it, though, like a two-headed nickel, the city called in the National Guard and the FBI and together with the city police they arrested and incarcerated most of both gangs and rendered the city safe at last. Because of Dylan Frye. He'd have to wait a period of time as things calmed down, but he could take credit for reducing the city's crime rate by several notches. All in a day's work. Not a problem.

Really.

7. The Office

During his high school years, Dyl spent his time busy doing other things rather than studying, not the least of which involved running for Student Council. Not only Student Council, but chair of the Student Council. The highest-ranking student office in the entire school, no matter the rank of the student in terms of freshman, sophomore, junior, or senior.

Dyl had never run for office before, but had many people he loved and who loved him back. So when it came time for him to make his plea to the election committee, he made it good. No script or notes to read from, only him and them, though he referred to himself always in the plural now meaning the royal 'we,' the impersonal 'we,' the 'we' that nurses often use when they ask how 'we are feeling today' when you're the only one otherwise in the room.

"'We love you for giving us this time to express our views. No, we really do. I mean really, *really* do. Thank you so much."

"That's it?" one member of the Council asked him.

"We're more interested in what you have to say than what we have to say."

"Okay, Dylan, what would you do first if you're elected to this office?"

"Good question. No, we mean it. A *really* good question. No pussy footing around. Get right to the point. We like that. We really, really do. Well, the most important thing that anyone would do in this kind of a position we're talking about here is to find out what's on the minds of those most affected by whatever you do. Get their opinions. Make a list."

"Okay, but don't you have any idea what your classmates have in mind? What they think is important for them at this point in their careers?"

"Another great question. Boy, you are full of great questions. Perfect ones, in fact. We have to give it to you for being on the ball. We're going to spread the word that you guys are for real."

"Well?"

"Well, what?"

"Do you have any idea what your classmates have in mind?"

"Sure."

"What?"

"First thing, I suppose, would be their curiosity about what we have in mind."

"So what do you have in mind?"

"Again. Another perfect question."

"Should be, I think it may be the fourth or fifth time I've asked it. Well?"

"Well, if what your saying is that what's on our mind is what's on theirs and what's on their minds is what's on ours, one of us will have to say something else."

"Yes, about what's on the docket as a plan for future activities."

"Future activities. Right. Perfect. Believe me when we say that these things are first and foremost on everyone's minds."

"Activities."

"Yes. You bet. Activities of many kinds."

"What kinds do you imagine?"

"All kinds. Not illegal kinds, mind you, but legal activities that the student body could imagine."

"Like what? Exactly?"

"Well any of the activities that we've had during the past year that everyone liked. Leave out the ones they didn't. You know. I mean who wants to go to an activity that had been proven unsuccessful? That wouldn't work. Yes sir, we're for activities that have proven successful, and by that I mean successful. Really successful. Successful activities for sure. No, I mean it. More of those."

"Such as?"

"Such as what?"

"What kinds of activities?"

"Successful activities?"

"Yes."

"Like?"

"Like dances and in-house carnivals, things like that."

"Exactly. Those would have been first out of my mouth. Dances and in-house carnivals. Great events. People really like those. Yes, for sure, dances and in-house carnivals. We negotiate those with the faculty, and by negotiate we mean *negotiate*. With Dylan you have someone who can truly negotiate and win. I like to win, believe me. Winning is important, maybe the most important part of this job. So dances and in-house carnivals we negotiate and win and have them, like the students want. See how it works?"

"What else?"

"What else, what?"

"Besides activities like dances and in-house carnivals."

"Could you be more specific?"

"Yes. Like more of a role in curriculum."

"Curriculum. Perfect. You guys are really something. I tell you we love you. The students love you. My God, the whole damn school loves you. Curriculum. Changes in curriculum. Yes."

"So what would you advise the students to ask for by way of changes in the curriculum?"

"Wow. Could you be more specific?"

"Like less requirements in the sciences and more in the arts? Less on football and sports and more on the sciences? Things like that."

"Of course. Perfect."

"Perfect what? Which would you choose?"

"Between what and what?"

"Well let's take a choice between the sciences and the arts as an example."

"Great question. It's the one we would have chosen if given a chance. Between science and the arts. By the arts we're guessing you mean art and music and theater and writing and dance and those things, right? Am I right?"

"Right. You are right."

"I'm assuming you're including mathematics, biology, chemistry, astronomy, geology, and so on for the sciences?"

"Yes. Absolutely."

"Boy, good subjects. No, I mean it."

"But which would you support?"

"Easy. What they wanted."

"Who wanted?"

"The students. We are a man of the people, you see. We represent the people, should we become Student Body President, that is. We're not a dictator like Mussolini. We are someone who works for the students in this process and let them express themselves through us as to what they want."

"Is that why you keep referring to yourself in the plural 'we?'"

"Have I done that? Wow, I guess I have. And yes, that's why I have. The students and I are together in this as we *should* be. I love them, all of them, and they me. Trust me. It works better that way. In the end, you'll see. My platform represents democracy for everyone."

"Thank you, Dylan."

"Am I done?"

"You are."

'Overdone,' whispered one of the council unheard by Dyl.

Dylan didn't win the election that year, nor the next, but he kept learning and by the time he'd reached his junior year he did win. By a landslide, and was reappointed by acclamation in his senior year, though that took two full years to complete. He'd failed, learned, and succeeded, in that order, an order that he aspired to from then on. Mostly, however, ever moving to the last word 'succeeded' as he grew older.

8. Graduation

Growing up without the support or presence of his parents had been an ordeal for Dylan. But they surprised him on his nineteenth birthday by showing up without warning for his high school graduation with him giving one of the student-choice speeches that day. He barely recognized either of them, dressed to the nines and hoping, too obviously so, to suggest to his friends' parents that they'd been by Dyl's side the whole nine yards of his youth.

"My fellow students, teachers, parents, and visitors, I welcome you to today's festivities." His opening seemed appropriate and unlike his usual style, but off the cuff nonetheless. "Thank you so much. This is so very nice today. Really nice. I mean that, I really do. As I came up to the podium today, I heard many people, many, many people, thousands of people, saying that this was a truly nice occasion, that they loved it. It's true. No, I mean it. Not a word said edgewise. Couldn't ask for a better day to have this kind of celebration of our wonderful lives in this free country. Though the world is collapsing around us at this very minute, collapsing yes. Believe it or not collapsing, we still live in a truly free country and should be proud of it. All of us proud of it. Truly proud. So that's the way it is. Very simple. Very simple indeed. But, of course, if the world's collapsing around us it means that we're collapsing as well. At least partially true that we're headed in some very wrong directions. Wrong directions. That's because some of us talk without action. We need more action and less talk. Am I right? Yes. I'm right. More action and less talk. We have to stand up for our rights. Right? Right. You know I'm right. We need to take action. Less talk and more action. Of course, there's the unthinkable. Yes, the unthinkable. Don't try to think about it because not only is it unthinkable, but thinking about it leads to talk and no action. Again, we need more action and, of course, it has to do with money. But, as you know, that's for a different conversation than this. Money. For a later time. Right now it's time for action. I'm sure you agree with that. We've never had this before. Never, ever had this before. That I can't talk about money, but only about action, and, of course, less talk. Isn't this a great day. So much love here. We love you and you us. A great day, I tell you. Look at you. In your going-to-meeting clothes. You look beautiful. Beautiful I tell you. Never been so beautiful. It's truly great to see you like this and your children who are no longer really children but in a kind of place somewhere between children and grownups. Maybe more grown up. It's a special time in a special country of the free. What a day, huh? What a great day. It's a game changer this day is. Let me tell you. A game changer. One hell of a game changer, let me tell you and pardon my French but I can't help it since it's such a great day. Again, thank you so much for giving me the opportunity to speak to you about these many important things. About talk, and action, and freedom, and about the future. Ah, the future. Who knows what it will bring? But come it will. No doubt about that. No doubt. Except maybe the world's imminent collapse. But that's for another time, the world's collapse. Now it's time for celebration and thank you so much for your love. I love you too. What a great day. Thank you, and I love you."

The large crowd of millions rose to their feet in unison and applauded Dylan's speech about things worth talking about and he realized that he, too, had a future full of important and improbable things. He had charisma and a way of cutting to the chase, delivering good and bad news in a manner that no one else could. Money and power would be his, if only he could stay on message and keep saying 'look' as often as he could. Keep reiterating 'at the end of the day' and things like 'beltway,' 'on the Hill,' 'fortune 500,' 'speaks volumes,' and 'the rustbelt,' he'd be fine.

His parents congratulated him before they rushed off to a flight to Uganda for which they could not give him a reason. Didn't matter, though, at least to Dylan, for he'd found a part of himself that day, a part he'd always knew existed but could not articulate, that he had himself to congratulate him. For real. Because himself was the only person he truly trusted.

9. A Brush With The Law

Knowing now of his skills at public speaking, Dylan decided to investigate the potentials of a career in law. If he could win the affections of parents at a huge graduation, he could surely win similar affections of juries. Of course he had little idea of the commitment it took to get a law degree and pass the bar, but for Dyl, such things didn't mean much. He'd tackle the most difficult of difficult things if it meant he could do what he wanted, and succeed at anything.

So, sooner than he could snap his fingers, he found himself working as a gofer for a law firm. This meant using one of his many bikes to take documents from one place to another and otherwise do most anything that no one else would touch. Demeaning work, yes, but it often put him within reach of the megabucks folks from whom he could listen and learn.

So, over weeks not years, he got the low down on subpoenas, hearings, dismissals, alimony, public defenders, appeals, sentences, arbitrations, testimonies, bail, summary processes, annulments, bench warrants, bonds, plea bargains, hearsays, briefs, felonies, continuances, affidavits, peremptory challenges, court reporters, damages, depositions, *voir dires*, detentions, plaintiffs, notarizations, dispositions, dockets, allegations, eminent domains, foremen, garnishments, hung juries, incarcerations, indigents, infractions, injunctions, interrogatories, jurisdictions, probations, liens, amicus curiae briefs, litigants, magistrates, counts, misdemeanors, motions, oaths, paroles, pleas, pre-trials, respondents, restitutions, calendars, stays, summonses, venues, and writs.

He further learned about those things not in the court's prerogative but still legally bound such as bail bondsmen, law firms, types of lawyers especially those who never set foot in courtrooms, lawsuits, serving gofers, class actions, settling out of court, postponements, and so on. Specialties like in Ford's assembly lines were the order of the day, and while beginning education started with law in general, one eventually specialized in one particular sub-sub-sub-field if one were to get anywhere.

None of this intimidated Dyl, of course, a man of many words but few fears. At the same time, not making money—certainly one of the more pronounced of those few fears—kept ringing in his ears as he worked for peanuts and saw nothing but years of more of the same in front of him before *maybe* making a living at best from his efforts. Not one of his enamored ambitions.

So, within six months of his joining the ranks of gofer at the law firm, Dylan took to the streets again— if you could call living rent free in his parents' mini-mansion taking to the streets—seeking another way up the ladder to success. Not depressed or despondent or feeling turned away, he plied his real trade, that of wooing through his pretended love for others to find, among the many amazing possibilities, the one prestigious profession that would grant him the fortune and fame that he wished above everything else in the world.

Of course, he found it. The love of his life. The most beautiful woman in the world and rich beyond the dreams of avarice. The daughter of a mega-millionaire and the center of attention in the upper-class world of the Big Apple by the name of Alicia Henderson. A definitely plain name, but definitely not a plain lady by any means and, as Dyl would eventually discover, someone equally enamored of dreams of power and wealth that staggered his own imagination.

10. True Love

Dyl saw Alicia Henderson for the very first time at a gala for the opening of a new art gallery on the eastside. Everyone who had any relationship to money in or around the greater metropolitan area of the great city had been invited, and the place was mobbed, crawling with people as Dylan would say, its space devoted to what he considered the newest of the newest of the new, a mess of supposedly shocking and appropriate ghastly mockups of Jackson Pollock's paintings and participatory multi-media from last century's sixties. The place smelled liked money. Not virtually, actually.

She'd stood in a corner saving herself the need to look at most of the walls and talking to a thin artist type about whatever such types had interest in and staring in Dyl's direction. She stood tall, from stilettos or true height he couldn't tell, and blonde, from dye or her own follicles he couldn't tell either, but gorgeous either way. He smiled, she smiled, and as far as Dylan could tell, the whole population of humankind smiled. So he took a stroll, tried to keep calm, and decided to introduce himself.

Dylan had always been a loner, but since he discovered his abilities to woo people by the thousands with his mental and vocal gymnastics, he'd gained a bravado that had served him well. So he interrupted Alicia Henderson and whomever by moving up beside her and said, not waiting for whomever to end his little speech, "I noticed you over here talking with him and thought I'd come over and say hello."

Whomever stopped midsentence and stared at Dyl as if Dyl had done something unforgiveable. "How dare you," the whomever said. Dylan, the inimitable Dylan, ignored the brat and pushed his way between the two conversationalists thereby ending the poor excuse for gossip, and held out his hand. Alicia glared at him and quickly added to the former's comment, "How dare you." Not original, obviously, but fine given the situation.

Dylan skipped that part and went right along to "My name is Dylan Frye, what's yours?"

Alicia was stunned by the audaciousness of her visitor and decided that she'd had enough. So she took the liberty to spill her Champagne glass, completely full at the time, over the front of Dylan's tuxedo and shirt front.

At first stunned and afterward quite taken with the action, Dyl said, "Thank you so much for that. It is rather warm in here, now that you mention it."

He caught a miniscule smile cross her lips but only for a second before she walked away, her derriere doing a dance for poor Dyl as he followed along the wall and nearly unhinging one of the Pollock imitations in doing so.

"I love this woman," he said to no one, and kept her in sight until she turned a corner and disappeared. Then he turned to the artist 'whomever' and asked, "Who was that woman?"

"You don't know?" the man asked.

"Now if I knew, why would I ask?"

"Alicia Henderson, and I saw her first."

"But I saw her second, and in this case, second gets the nod."

"She's mine," whomever argued.

"Why you?" Dyl asked in return.

"She's rich."

"The hell with that," Dyl said, "I want in her pants. You can have her money."

Whomever, obviously wanting out of this ridiculous conversation, gave it some thought, figured they could both get what they wanted if they played their cards right, and stuck out his hand to shake Dyl's. They agreed to disagree, and agreed to agree, depending on the aim of each in terms of what they wanted to accomplish.

Later and after he'd left the party, Dyl, apparently, got the upper hand by calling a friend from high school who owed him a favor and to give him Alicia's unlisted home phone number, with cell phones not available at the time, and he called her the next morning.

"Hello, Alicia?" Dyl said, after verbally crawling through three different maids and butlers and conning them into letting him speak to the apparent princess.

"Who's this?" she asked, with a definite negative tone to her voice for being interrupted.

"The person you spilled Champagne upon last night at the grand opening of the new gallery in town."

She hung up on him.

'What a beginning,' he whispered aloud before he could breathe again. Clearly love at its finest.

He dialed the rotary dial a second time and got the same runaround through which he negotiated with aplomb.

With the same result. This time before he got around to saying her name.

"I love this woman," Dyl said, this time so anyone within hearing range, which no one was at the time, could hear.

He dialed her number a third time, this time, no one answered. Obviously by order of the madam of the house. At least at this time of day.

Dyl therefore, making up his mind not to dwell on lost causes, dressed himself as well as he could, plead the address of his blond love from another high school friend, took his father's BMW north to where Alicia lived, gave up trying to decode the lock on the metal fence's gate, leapt the thing after several attempts to sneak through the bars, went to the door, and gave the knocker there several swings before one of the maids from earlier answered.

"I'm here to see Miss Henderson," he said, "Miss Alicia Henderson, if you please."

It didn't make this particular maid pleased, possibly recognizing his voice from over the phone earlier, but she asked anyway, "Is she expecting you?"

"She is," Dyl lied right out.

"Whom may I say is calling?"

"Not calling, I'm here. Right here. My name is Dylan Frye. She already knows me." Before she knew it, Dyl had placed his foot in the door making it impossible for the diminutive maid to lock him outside. After pushing the door open a bit further, he walked inside and took a seat on a chair near the stairs down which he assumed Alicia, his Alicia, would come to meet him, unable to not since he was already inside.

When she didn't immediately appear, Dyl took a magazine from a table for such near him and leafed through it. A catalog for dinner wear and various associated fine clothing. The prices made him wince. A thousand here, a couple thousand there, and so on, things he thought his long ago group of 'buy from the poor and sell to the rich' could get for a few dollars and launder into a tiny fortune.

He may have missed her approach, but not her appearance, for she stood about four feet away from Dyl in a white dress so short that he could swear he could see her lack of underwear.

"What the hell are you doing here?" she asked him. "Whatever your name is."

"Dylan Frye, Miss Alicia, at your service."

"I thought you came from wealth, Mister Frye, now you act like someone looking for a job as my car scrubber."

"You look like a breath of fresh air on a planet with no atmosphere," Dyl replied, using the entirety of his metaphoric responses.

"Forget it, buster, your idiocy is lost here. Now get out before I have you thrown out."

She turned to leave, but Dylan reached out and gently turned her slightly back toward him.

"Not so fast," he said. "You should hear me out to make sure you're not making a mistake."

She stared at him with a combination of malice and curiosity. A good combination, he thought. One he liked.

But she didn't leave or attempt to turn again, giving him the chance he needed.

"Listen, Alicia, and I mean this, I really do. You are the most beautiful woman in the world. Without the slightest doubt. Beautiful, believe me. You really are. Besides that, however, you're the one. I mean, *the one*. I'm going places. I really am. Many places. Thousands of places that represent the future. Not only my or your future, but everyone's futures. You can take that to the bank, and you *will* take it to the bank if we join together for the adventure of a lifetime. Listen, you're the greatest, I mean the greatest woman I've ever met. By the way, I'm the greatest man you've ever met. Our getting together is in the stars. No really, it is. In the stars. Truly in the stars. We're made for one another. Now, I know this is sudden and you don't really know who I am yet, but if you'll come to dinner with me tonight and really get to know me, you'll see the truth that is me. I really mean it."

Alicia stared at him in disbelieve. Dyl wasn't sure why, but she did. Apparently she could resist his charm and charisma, his manner of speaking the truth, of introducing her to a new life of excitement and challenge, one and the same as he saw it.

"Get the hell out of here," she told him.

"Listen. Don't get me wrong. A dinner, and I'll be happy to pay. Wherever you want to go. Doesn't matter the cost. You and me. I won't get fresh, I promise you. Don't you believe me? Believe me, please. I don't lie, ever. Lying. Not in my vocabulary. Just good food and friendly talk. You and me. Please? You're the center of my universe. Yes. You are. Never has anyone been so perfect as you. Believe me. I never lie. How about it?"

"What's with you, anyway?"

"What's with me, is you, Alicia. You. Nothing but you. Did you know that? I mean before I told you. I bet you didn't, and if you don't know a place, a good place for us to eat tonight I mean, I know of many. We'll have a stunning time. A stunning time, I tell you. A really stunning time. I have to say that a lot of people have been asking about me and you. Yes, it's true. Many people. Hundreds of people if you must know. I tell them that you are the greatest, Alicia, and you are. The greatest. I want to spend a little time with you and tell you about my plans, and, of course, listen to your plans. I'd like to hear those plans. I really would. You've got to understand how important you are to me. Really."

She kept staring at him, looking like she'd entered some kind of catatonic state, put into a waking sleep as she'd listened to his speech.

"Where?" she asked him, and before she knew it she had a date with Dylan Frye and would meet him at her door that evening at seven to go to the place of his choosing to eat what he'd described as the meal of her lifetime. Together they'd talk about the future not only of the two of them, but the entire world, and his and her places in that world. 'Who was this guy?' she asked herself silently on her way up the stairs, and what was he suddenly doing in her life? Certainly not the man of her dreams, but somehow the man of the moment.

At least that.

11. Engagement

As much as Dylan wanted 'in her pants' as whomever had said at the gala, Dylan also wanted to marry the woman of his dreams. He wanted her beside him when he did whatever he was going to do with his life, and she was the perfect one to stand there with him, showing the world how successful he really was. So he spent the first part of dinner, the waiting, the ordering, eating the first course, and so on, asking her questions, smiling, and most importantly listening to her talk about her own dreams and her own aspirations. Actually listening. Really. He wanted to know the keys that would open her up to him and make what he wanted possible. It was only two thirds of the way through the main course that she asked him much the same question as he'd asked her at the beginning. About his dreams and aspirations.

"Me?" he said, fearful his simple response might give him away. Truthfully as he always worried he might.

"Yes, dummy, you. What are you so impossibly interested in that you'd think I'd care about it?"

"Me, huh? You want to know about me?"

"I do. Before you run out of time."

"I'm on the clock am I?"

"You are."

"Okay, I'd better get to it. I have a dream as well. Mine is simpler than yours. Very simple. You might think it too simple."

"I will if you never getting around to telling me."

"I want to marry you and live the rest of my life with you."

"You do, do you?"

"See, that was perfect. A palindrome without giving it thought. You do, do you? A perfect palindrome. You're incredible."

"Stop with the horseshit, will you, and tell me what you wanted to tell me this morning. About your dreams and inspirations. About the future that you said would be so incredible. The future that would make us world famous or something like that."

"Listen, it will work. All you need, not you specifically, but us who will convert many to our ideas, many millions. Billions maybe. Sure, billions. Why not? Is that we lay out our agenda for everyone to see. Transparency. Clear intentions for everyone to see and understand. From there the world's our oyster. See what I mean?"

"No."

"Well, let me explain it this way. Make myself clearer. This will help. We need to address the problems we face in attaining power and money. Power and money. Those two things. We get those and we're on our way."

"I already have those."

"Yes you do. But compared to the top one percent, you have only a small amount of those. We need to address that issue."

"So, we want more power and more money?"

"Sure. That's it, exactly. As much as possible, and once we have those two things we can address our needs, and equally so the needs of others. It's really a good cause. No, it is. Really. Everyone benefits from this. That's how we get the power and money. See. Because others will understand that it's for them as well as for us. A lot of people have come up to me and ask these kinds of questions, and I tell them that unless you have power and money you can't get anywhere with these issues. They agree with me. Many people. Hundreds of people. Thousands. They can see how it works. They're telling us, you and me, how to do it. That they want us to do it for them. Do you see?"

"Not really."

"Listen. At the end of the day, these people speak volumes about what we're both after. The pot at the end of the rainbow and the manner in which we'll share that pot. When we find it, that is. Sure. That's it. Really, it's the way it's done. You know what I mean? It's not easy, of course, but with two people like us, with the drive, the means, the mutual respect, and so on, we can't miss."

"So you want more power and money?"

"Well, those and you."

"Why do you need me?"

"Because with you at my side I'm completely convinced that I will be successful. One look at you and, of course, listening to you as well. Don't forget that, people will listen carefully and understand how it works and go for it. Believe me, they will."

The table fell quiet for a minute.

"I'm not sure what to say," Alicia said.

"Maybe you need time to think about it?" Dylan asked her.

"No, I know what I think, but I don't know what to tell you. That's it."

"Do you need more information?"

"Not so much, no. I think I've pretty much understood what you have to say."

"You do? Everything's a go?"

"No. No go."

"Why not?"

"Because, you idiot, you haven't told me anything. Anything. Except, of course, that you'd like to have me and that you'd like to have more power and money as everyone would. Those and the rest of your words are as vacuous as your head apparently is."

For once, Dylan was speechless. Absolutely speechless. What a woman. He couldn't imagine any woman more beautiful, smart, and decisive as she. He had to have her. In every way possible. He had to. What could he say to her to make that happen?

"Would you marry me?" he said abruptly. "I don't have a ring to offer you at this moment, but I could get one by tomorrow morning. I mean it, I could get down on my knees and present it to you as properly as one can present a ring to anyone. I mean it. I really do. I could make you happy by giving you anything and everything you've ever wanted. You don't have to respond to me at this moment, but maybe in the next week or so. You can turn me down and I won't take it personally as long as you let me keep on asking you until I say yes. You see, you're like me in so many ways. No, your are. You tell the truth. You don't hold back doing it either. You're the greatest. You really are. The greatest. The most perfect person on earth. I love you with every fiber of my soul. I do. I really do. What do you say?"

"I can't believe what I said and what you said go together in any rational way. I barely know your name. You promise me the world with no specifics on how you're going to get it. You talk like a madman. A narcissistic madman. Arrogance is a word created for amateurs. You're a professional flimflam artist who makes the words arrogance and guile seem like synonyms. Easy cousins. What the hell makes you tick, anyway?"

"You do, Alicia. You do."

"A repetition, not a palindrome. Get the car, asshole, and take me home."

"I love you, I really do," Dyl said as he followed orders. "Can I come over in the morning and see you?"

It cost Dylan two restraining orders and one arrest over the first month of their so-called courtship, at least Dyl called it that, before he saw Alicia up close again at her house.

"What are *you* doing here?" she asked him.

"To tell you that you're the most exciting person in the world, and that I come in a close second."

"What?"

"Think of it, Alicia, what a beautiful name to go with such a beautiful woman, how the last month would have been if you weren't so busy avoiding me, getting restraining orders from the court, and having me arrested. Admit it. I'm the most interesting person you've ever met. No, I mean it. Give it some thought. Look, we're meant for each other. I haven't seen you in a month and you're still the most interesting person in the world to me. Believe me when I tell you that we're absolutely meant for one another."

He wanted to continue, but the cops arrived and dragged him away to the county jail for another over-nighter. For Dyl, though, it was a sign of pure love on her part. But it also meant another month before he'd see her again.

Before they did, however, Alicia screamed "Shit!" Aren't you ever going to give this up?"

"How can I? That's the way it is. Simple. You have my love whether you think you want it or not. Plus, it's forever, I tell you. Forever. Really, forever. I respect and adore you, and you me whether you know it or not. What you're doing I can understand. You can't help it. Maybe in your place I couldn't help it either. You're afraid of commitment, Alicia. Everyone is. I have but one goal. To make you happy. Really. One goal. Happy. Forever happy. That's it, Alicia. How can you resist that?"

"You could make me really happy, you know that?"

"How?"

"By getting the hell away from me and staying away. You're driving me nuts."

"That's so good to hear. Many people say that to me. Many of them. Hundreds. But no one can say it like you do. You're driving me nuts, too."

"Go away."

"Not before you let me continue you to talk to you."

"Saying what to me?"

"That I love you. That I want to marry you. That I want us to live happily ever after as rich and famous people. I'll never let you down, Alicia. Never. Believe me when I say that. Never. Do you believe me?"

"No."

"No? I am not a liar, Alicia. I never lie. This is important. Important in the sense that you believe me. I'll never let you down. Excitement every minute. No, really. One hundred percent of the time. You can ask anyone I've ever known if I lie. They'll tell you I don't. Ever. Believe me when I tell you that. Hundreds of people you can ask. Maybe thousands. Yes, thousands."

"What do you want, Dylan?"

It was the first time he could remember her using his name in a conversation. A special moment. A moment of his lifetime he'd never forget.

"Can we go upstairs and you let me talk with you about anything you want to talk about?"

"After the cops take you away, damn, I guess so. I'll follow you down to the station and pick you up there."

With that, the frozen ice broke at the North Pole and she and Dylan made up. He got inside her pants and they eventually got married, an event that no one could believe no less understand. But it happened. No, believe me, it really did.

12. Death And Real Estate

While still engaged, Dylan heard some disturbing news. His parents, the ones he rarely saw and when he did rarely stayed around long enough for him to speak with them, died in a plane crash in Portugal. Not any plane crash, mind you, but one to light up the skies over Lisbon. It would quickly be labeled a mid-east terrorist act leaving nothing but a few pieces scattered over many miles as evidence. Not a single whole body could be found among the two hundred passengers and crew, but the dust left from the explosives proved the source.

    The funeral Dyl mounted for his parents was embarrassingly brief for several reasons. First, his anger at never having had a relationship with them had left him holding that proverbial bag of lost hopes. Second, that he didn't want to waste any of his own money. Third, their wills had not yet announced who or whom would be the inheritors of their wealth. If not him, he would be out on his own without a home to live in with his engaged and now no doubt enraged wife to be. This was inexcusable to him. As was his entire familial situation since he'd been born.

    For once, though, things turned out to his advantage. His mommy and daddy had left him with everything. Since his Nanny and maid had quit as Dylan had grown beyond his needing them, they weren't mentioned in the will and thus no competition for the two's mini-fortune and mansion.

It was now Dylan's property and for that he thanked his lucky stars. Since his own saved-up dough from his exploits during high school had been eaten up during his trials and tribulations as a law gofer, this was a perfect ending to a vacuous parental relationship.

Alicia and Dyl's wedding, paid for in full by the bride's parents as tradition demanded, involved one of those ministers who achieved their low-budget status by paying a few bucks to a bogus religion that had properly dodged the right laws and answered the questions fully, dolling out credentials like candy to babies. The preacher attended wearing shorts and a tee shirt and boasted no denomination of any kind that anyone could tell. Didn't matter though. It was good enough for the Hendersons who held no particular beliefs along these lines and secretly hoped Alicia would dump this joker and marry someone of actual importance in the city, either by divorce or, better, by termination via annulment.

Instead, however, Alicia's parents received the news that their daughter was pregnant, clear proof of Dyl, or at least someone, had gotten into her pants, with a due date at least a month earlier than that of nine months since the wedding.

The couple, with their now daily battles, celebrated the little one, whom they'd later discover was to be a boy, and life turned from daily spats to fights over who would go out at two in the morning to buy tutti-frutti ice cream.

During this time, and maybe especially during this time, Dylan decided to take a chance on real estate to enlarge their fortune and to get the hell away from the woman of his dreams. No better way to do that than by the odd and long hours required of a real estate agent or broker or whatever. Of this profession he knew little except that one could make money at it and sometimes with very little work involved. Of course, having a gift for gab and for embellishing the truth didn't hurt either.

Turned out, Dyl faced four hurdles, the first two of which he'd already hurdled, those being eighteen years of age or older and being a U.S. resident. The next two, though, not quite so easy. But not that hard either. He had to complete a required pre-license education either online or at a school, he chose school to escape his mini-mansion, and take his state's real estate license examination that that education prepared him for.

By wising up his teacher to his already non-existent knowledge of real estate buying and selling, he got out of school with only twice as much studying and time as most did and passed the exam itself by flying within a single point of failing. Didn't matter, though, since passing was passing. The only thing that mattered. Within a couple of months of making his decision, he was interviewing with brokers who would take him on as a temp until he proved his worth. This, many months yet before his first-born would arrive and snarl up his availability and flexibility.

Less than a week after his mug shot had been planted on the walls of the broker's establishment and in their pamphlet customers could see and choose their agents from, Dyl got his first bite and had been assigned a two-million dollar coastal unit on the shores south of Atlantic City in the town of Longport southeast of Atlantic Avenue. A beautiful townhouse with perfect views and not that far from his own home, so he knew the area well and could rack up points.

When Dylan told Alicia, his beloved, her reaction, especially since he'd lied and said he'd been out with the boys and not acquiring a real-estate license, things did not go that well.

"What the fuck?" she screamed at him. "How dare you lie to me, you shithole."

All these words appear in English dictionaries everywhere, but having your pregnant yet newly married wife, the woman of your dreams, yelling them at you during a moment of celebration, did not quite line up with Dyl's vision of his dream girl.

So, without hesitation, he said, "Up yours, bitch, it's what I'm going to do for us and you'd better get used to it you motherfucker." Other good words in the same dictionary, but unexpected nonetheless.

His real-estating went much better, though, as the first couple he showed the townhouse to appeared interested, especially when Dyl told them of various appliances like washers, driers, dishwashers, and so on, which would be added without cost before the sale, saving them a bundle in addition to the great price the owners were asking. He left out the constant flooding of the basement during storm conditions. It wasn't fair to make such an eager pair sad at this point in the sales process.

When the pair unfortunately decided on another place in which to sink their money and Dyl lost his sale to another agent, he gained necessary experience of the 'buy,' and knew it would aid him in future dealings. He also knew that in New Jersey, selling four such places a year gained him a salary of over one hundred grand and after that it was gravy.

So he took the next couple interested in the Longport townhouse to view the property, and opened his spiel with a decidedly different approach. A hard to get idea he'd had when not listening to Alicia nag him about something or other.

"You gotta understand, folks, that this is prime property in this area and that many couples are interested in buying this particular place. No, really, there are. I mean many couples. Dozens of them. Maybe a hundred. It's hard to describe to you how I've had to keep them from laying their money right on the line the minute they see it. Believe me, what a place. It'll knock you right out of your socks, I tell you. At the end of the day, you're going to love it. I mean 'love it.'"

"Huh?" the husband of the pair asked.

"He telling us that lots of people want this place and we will love it as well."

"Huh," the husband of the pair said.

"She's right, that exactly what I said. I love the way you put it. So carefully and accurately put. I mean right on the button. Listen, it's also got a price tag that's way under the market value, let me tell you. Way under. Way, way under, and here it is. Right on time. See what did I tell you? The perfect place. Three stories, ocean view, privacy, your own property,

definitely not a condo. A real place of your own. Right?
I mean it, I really do. I never lie about such things.
Never. Believe me."

"Huh?" the husband of the pair asked.

"He says that it's cheap."

"No, not cheap. Inexpensive. A bargain. The
owners wish to sell it quickly to pay for the other
home they've already bought, you see. No, really. It's
more than a deal, it's a steal. Not really a steal, of
course, but it will seem like one once you get inside
and see how homey and comfortable it is."

"Can we see inside?" the wife of the pair asked.

"Of course you may. Follow me and I'll not only
show you around, but answer any questions you ask
to boot."

"A bargain, he says?" the husband of the pair
said.

"Okay dear. He's trying to help."

"Help, smelt, he's trying to unload a lemon."

"Now dear. Give him a chance."

"One. One chance. One, I tell you. No, really.
Believe me."

"Stop it, dear."

Dylan had never been parroted before, and he
liked it. Made him feel important and maybe a little
trusted. He went on to tell them about everything but
the basement flooding, answered their questions
including the suspicious husband's ones, and when
they left, neither had said the unmagical word 'no.' No
'maybes' either, or the slightest optimistic 'nice' or
'good views.' So, though they eventually opted for a
more opulent place at half the price, he had made a

step forward rather than backward, he felt, and sat in his closet for an office and gave the picture more thought. What was he missing here? What could he added to his spiel that would get him over the hump of selling his first property? It took a while, but he ultimately got an idea. Tell them what they wanted to hear. For that, he had to ask them questions. Take the answers he got and make the place appear to have everything they ever wanted in a new place to live. Why he hadn't thought of this first confused him, but he had thought of it eventually, and, because it would take a lot of the energy to shut the 'fuck' up, he could do it, hear the magic words his potential customers said, and give them what they wanted. Even if he had to gild the Lilly a bit and fudge with his answers.

Thus, the next couple that asked him to show them the place he listened to. Had to ask them a question or two to get things started, but once begun they couldn't stop themselves. After all, everyone loves to talk about themselves and what they want.

"What exactly are you looking for," he initiated his first query.

Off they went. Everything from this kind of bathroom, that kind of kitchen, those kinds of staircases, that variety of chandelier, that color of paint, and so on. With each, he answered with short replies like, 'no problem,' or 'easily done,' or 'faster than a flying bullet,' and on and on. Of course, he was flim-flamming them a bit around the edges since most of what he promised they'd have to do themselves, but what did it matter, the broker would get to those after the deal was essentially sealed. Easy.

When they ran out of questions, Dylan did his best not to overdo his own spiel and basically followed the dictum that 'less was more,' something he found difficult to accomplish but wanted the sale, something to tell Alicia about and gloat over the money he'd made. The beginning of the fortune he would soon earn.

Included was his determination to tell the big truths, which in this case was the basement flooding. Not to bring it up, mind you, but at least to admit it if the subject arose.

"What about the basement?" the wife of the pair asked. "Does it leak?"

"Yes. Not the reason the previous owners left because it happens rarely, but it does leak."

"See?" she told her husband. "He doesn't lie."

"Yeah, yeah. But does it ever flood?"

"Yes. But only in major storms such as hurricanes losing their paths down south. Rare, but it happens."

"See?" he told his wife. "Told you so."

This couple didn't buy the house either. Tell the truth, no go. Fudge a little, and no go. Either way, a bust. Maybe Dylan had to find a slot somewhere near the middle. A little fibbing and a little truth.

Six weeks before their baby came due and the house having not sold yet after more than twenty couples had visited it and turned the sale price down, Dylan was desperate. Not because they couldn't afford the best doctors and the best hospital for their first child's delivery unto this world, but because Dyl couldn't stand Alicia's constant badgering any longer.

With that understood, Dyl approached his twenty-fourth couple in desperation.

"Listen," he said, "I gotta tell you, this place is a honey. It ain't perfect, but if you like townhouses the view is to die for and it's within walking distance of the center of town, in the best neighborhood, I mean everyone's great around here, and, between you and me, we can sell it for less than we're asking. No, I mean it. I have to say this, I really do, you'll regret not giving it a go around. What do you say?"

The wife of the couple nodded.

"Good. Now, I'm going to give you the keys and stay out here and watch the surf as you take a tour. Collect your questions as you do and give them to me after you're through, okay?"

"Okay," the husband of the couple said, with something like a sigh of relief as he did.

Dylan waited. He'd tried several times doing it every way else he could think of and nothing had worked. He couldn't imagine this would either as it defied every hint he'd learned in getting his license, but what the hell, give it a chance.

When the couple exited the front door, the husband nodded. No questions. Within a few days the sale was settled and Dylan had made his first sale of a house in his life. Money and power, at least the first glimpse of them beyond what his parents had died and left him, were his. Real estate was easy. Do nothing. The one thing no one had thought to tell him.

13. Marriage

Dyl endured Alicia's glandular temper tantrums and somehow they remained married at least until the baby—name of Quinn, by the way, for no known reason either one of them could imagine since neither had a single red corpuscle of Irish blood in their veins—was born. Eight pounds of screaming, wriggling, and constantly hungry baby boy ready to drive his parents crazy. Dyl easily now understood why his parents had abandoned him so early in life. He immediately got in touch with his former nanny to see if she was available and still alive after these many months.

Alicia hated breast-feeding and quickly warmed to the idea of a nanny as well, so Dyl's still-alive nanny came home to where she'd spent so many years to raise yet another Frye from birth to mid-teens. Alicia went back to crabbing about everything. Dyl returned to keeping long hours at the office and as much as possible taking potential customers to various ritzy homes that no one else at the brokerage could sell.

And sell those houses he did. A lot he left them to decide on their own, but, it turned out, couples were different as peanuts in a jar. Some needed hand holding, some wanted lies, some wanted truth, some wanted to talk, some wanted him to talk, some wanted views, some wanted pink walls, others black walls, who knew? He did. Turned out he had a knack for quickly determining which type each couple was before they opened their mouths. Young, old, didn't matter. He had it nailed. By the time Quinn was one and Alicia and Dyl had worked out the details of the divorce, Dylan had sold nine homes, each worth more than the previous, that no one else in the brokerage firm would take on or could sell. He made well over a quarter of a million during his first year and knew he'd hit the jackpot of professions.

When Alicia hit the road with her parents screaming for joy, Quinn in hand without any connections to Dylan who was glad to be rid of the pains in the ass, and Dylan nearly cleaned out except for his mini-mansion and most of what his parents had left him in inheritance, Dyl had moved up to a different brokerage, a different aged clientele, and a larger portion of the take. He'd learned many lessons over the year with Alicia, the biggest being don't marry someone because you want in their pants, marry them because you love them. Or at least want to love them if you're incapable of love in the first place.

His new clientele included Atlantic City's version of the mob. The Big Apple's less fortunate version. Guys that Dylan understood but had aversion for. They'd rubbed out those who did them wrong and, given their free interpretations of doing them wrong on any given day, meant that he'd taken one step up the ladder financially, and two back in terms of staying alive.

His new products, though, proved more than substantial enough. No more townhouses. Buildings. Some of many stories, both stories as in first, second, third, with no thirteen, and stories as in short stories and long stories, the latter told by members of the community and usually involved with making those living in those buildings paying their rents on time or else. Luckily, though, not his job. His job, sell the suckers as fast as he could to the next entrepreneur of exploitation. Not so tough given that the previous absentee owner had provided a perfect template for the new owner to follow. Stay the hell away from your investment regardless of what the contract says. Buy it, rake in the dough, keep the thugs intimidating the tenants to get the rent paid, and let the thing fall apart hoping to get as much from the place as you could before it emptied out or the building completely fell apart. Not Dyl's problem. His was to sell the places, take his cuts, and run.

He had to change his spiel, though. His customers had changed, and from young married couples to self-aggrandized billionaires who more than slightly adhered to making more money no matter the cost to their ethics, a word that few of them knew existed.

"Wow, I can't believe it, you're here with me. Alone. The two of us. You're amazing, you know that? Truly amazing. I've heard so many great things. No, I really have. This is not bull I'm telling you. I'm not exaggerating in the least. No exaggeration. Look at you. Just look at you. The man everyone looks up to. A perfect gentleman. Have I got a deal for you. Amazing, I tell you. Absolutely amazing. You won't believe it, let me tell you. An amazing deal for an amazing man. A perfect match. Really."

Back to his old ways, but for the most part it worked. When it didn't, he changed gears and returned to his married-your-first-house patter. If that didn't work, he had fifteen others, one of which was certainly bound to cut the mustard. Of course, many if not most of the potential deals were handled by lesser ups than the main man, rough and tumble guys down the ladder a ways and ready and willing to cut the crap by pulling a switchblade and carving up the agent, Dyl in this case, for lunch.

But Dylan always found something that would do it and kept his vital parts in one piece. His knowledge of street language helped. He'd also nailed most of the hand signals and body language that worked to his advantage. Hands up when the knife appeared, keeping at least an arms distance from his client when talking, and having clearly scoped out wherever he was for quick exits.

Occasionally he had to accompany a potential buyer to what Dyl was selling, an interesting trip to say the least. The places were rat infested, covered in graffiti, windows protected by metal bars at least on the ground floors and those floors within throwing distance of bricks from the sidewalks, and surrounded by addicts, dealers, prostitutes, drunks, pickup stickball games, and gangs in cars playing 'chicken' in the streets.

But Dyl made it work, sold a few which in this case meant double his income from the townhouse racket, and he got promoted and his office doubled in size along with his clientele improving to the more upscale rackets of Wall Street buyers and sellers and billionaires instead of mere millionaires.

14. The True Realtor

When he made top sales in his bracket one year, Dyl knew the top level was in reach. That level, when he arrived, meant selling buildings, yes, but not the tenant type, but the one-owner type with the owner's name attached to whatever the building, new most of the time, was called. As in Frye Towers, he imagined, across from Central Park in the Big Apple with a view of the lakes and the rapes and the robberies and Shakespeare during the summers.

When he raked in enough dough and spread his name around the proper circles, he quit his relatively new firm and opened up his own one-realtor company in Atlantic City to save on rent and attract his own business, one in which he took both takes, the one for realtor and the one for broker. Double the money, with rent for his office not an issue since he'd bought the place outright.

It never occurred to Dylan to miss his ex-wife and son. He'd figured when they split that that was that on both and that he'd always look forward and never back except for paving the way for the future. A divorce, certainly, was in no way useful as a positive step for the next thing in his life, so he forgot all about it. He'd done fine without parents, so could his son.

Dyl made everything positive. Turn lead into gold. Alchemy. Metaphysics. Nothing gained by going south when you lose, always turn north. In some ways, this became one of those gotcha moments for

Dylan. An epiphany. A joyous moment of knowing that whatever happened it was perfect. Didn't take a genius to figure it out. Not in the least. Positive was far better than negative, especially when it came to matters of business. If you couldn't make the deal, make the deal come to you. There was no way that wouldn't work, he thought, and, like many of the things Dyl had tried, it was that that turned his life from a slow road to China into a fast road to Shangri-La.

"Listen, it doesn't work. It really doesn't work. No way. Can you believe it, these crackerjacks you been working with think it works, but it doesn't. It doesn't work. They'll never learn. Never. Now me, I know what works. Absolutely I do. Check it out on the Internet. Check it out. Believe me when I tell you I know what works. I really do. This building we're talking about here, it's the likes of which you've never seen before. Well, maybe you've seen it from afar, but not up close. Everybody loves it. They love it. I love it. I really do, and so will you when you've seen it. It's unbelievable. Unbelievable. People are endlessly telling me about it. Every bit of it. Endless. Lots of people. Hundreds of people, thousands maybe. Thousands. They know. Truly they know. So let's go and see your future, shall we? Your future. It's not often that one gets to see their future like this. Not often. But you're going to see it, right in front of your eyes. Truly. You're going to love this. Love it, I tell you. I won't lie to you. Never lie. My mother taught me that. No lying. You're going to love it."

"Price's a bit steep isn't it?"

"Forget the price for now. Now it's time for you to tell me whether you want it or not. Then we'll talk price. You're gonna love this part. You really will. You're a perfect match for this beautiful building and it for you. A match made in heaven, I tell you. No, I really mean it. Never lie about such things. Wait until you see the rooms. Not only the layout and the size, but the entire setup. The furnishings. Perfect for a man of your taste and, of course, your patrons. Imagine as I walk you through what it'll look like in a brochure. Online. To your guests when they open the doors. Unbelievable, that's what they'll think. Unbelievable. Can you believe it will be yours?"

"It is lovely."

"They're all like that. Trust me. Every one of them. Let's see, shall we. I'll take you next door. You'll see. Unbelievable."

Dyl had made the two that he showed perfect in every way. The rest, not so much. No more low level types scratching their crotches and looking like gorillas in suits. These were the top dogs, so high on the ladder that they didn't know themselves what was going on to keep them there. These guys didn't know about the DEAL. Everything they knew was that they were the top dogs and that everyone below them did their bidding.

When it came to the DEAL, Dyl didn't disappoint. Grab your clients by the balls, and they'll follow you anywhere.

"Listen, you like this place, don't you? I mean what a place, right?"

"Yes, but the asking price is way to high."

"So what's the price you want to pay?"

"About twenty percent less."

"Not bad. But I'd buy it if it were that. Never show it around. Believe me when I say that others have offered more than that right off. You have a second shot in the dark?"

"Fifteen percent lower, maybe."

"That's only a ten million loss for me. I gotta tell you, I was expecting a much better offer from you. Not what I'm asking, mind you, that's too much. But the builder, the guy who put up the splash in the first place, I'd still have to pay him a bunch. You remember the places we saw on your first visit?"

"Sure."

"Perfect weren't they?"

"Sure."

"They're all that way. I mean it. But it's no big deal. Look, you've been straight with me and I've been straight with you. I love you for that. We love you for that. So no big deal. I'll either sell it to one of those with the higher offers or keep trying. Hell, it's worth it to see such a beautiful hotel go to the right person. Of course, I thought you were that person. I'm not exaggerating, believe me. No, I mean it. This is the best thing I've ever put on the market. The very best thing. I'm proud of it. As if it were my own, you know? I'll find a buyer. Hell, I still may buy it myself."

"You'd really buy it?"

"I'm in the business. Been in the business for a long time. You got to play it straight with your customers, right? Well I'm playing it straight. This beauty is worth every penny. I'm not exaggerating."

"I believe it."

"Good. Because it's true. Right down to the nuts and bolts in the walls holding it together. First rate. Everything. So thank you very much for putting up with my gab, and I'll let you go back to your business and maybe see you again on some other project. No harm, no foul, as they say."

"I'm sorry."

"Don't be. Tomorrow someone will stop by and wham, it'll be theirs. Like that, I tell you. Like that. Exactly like that. It happens sometimes. I hope you don't drive by and see their name in lights at the top under the towers up there and get mad at yourself for not taking it when you had the chance. Think you could have had it for a song but didn't take it."

"A song?"

"When you think about it. Hell the thing will be eventually worth ten times what whoever buys it will pay. Ten times. My guess, though, will be that their love for it won't let them sell. Even with everyone begging that owner to sell it."

"I never did get the price you'd sell it for. I mean the price lower than the one advertised."

"The price advertised is the lowest price anyone will ever pay. No discounts."

"I thought you said you'd provide a discount."

"I did. The listed price is many more millions lower than the price I was going to list if for. I couldn't talk the current owner into going up. As it is, he's allowing me less than one percent commission on this baby. Less than. Believe me, that took a big bite out of my yearly income, let me tell you."

"If you sell it."

"Oh, I'll sell it. Already have bids in at that price."

"Why didn't you take them?"

"Couldn't. Or maybe wouldn't would be the better word."

"Why not?"

"They weren't the right guys. You see, when I sell buildings of this fundamental quality, I don't do it for the money. I do it for the love. Love is the right word. I'm a matchmaker. A matchmaker is the right word. Can you believe it? It's true, I tell you. Only the best for Frye's customers. Only the best. Nothing but the best. I love my job. Believe me I love my job, and when you love your job, you can't let a little money get in the way of things."

"I understand."

"I know you do. I truly know you do. I can see it in your eyes and in everything you do. That's why I picked you for this sale over the others, and there are many of them. You, however, are different."

Dyl sold the building to the guy. At list price. Upped his commission by eight million for a few measly words.

Amazing.

15. Sleep

Dylan suffered often from nightmares during this time. So much so, that he slept maybe three hours a night and often found himself staying up to avoid another bout of being chased, flying around without wings, and watching someone being butchered and not doing anything about it.

"Do you know, Mister Frye, that you've mentioned the word 'I' and the word 'We' exactly twenty-six times each during the last hour?" the psychiatrist said to Dyl at the end of his first visit.

"This have to do with my nightmares?" he asked back.

"I don't know. But it does have to do with your general mental health that at least indirectly relates to your nightmares. See how that works?"

"No. But go on ahead."

"Well, two issues come to mind here. First is the same number twenty-six. Exactly the same. Second, these words indicate a preoccupation with yourself."

"Isn't everyone preoccupied with themselves?"

"Certainly. To a degree, at least. At the same time, you've not mentioned anyone else but yourself during the past hour. Since you've entered this office, actually, with the exception of me, someone you can't help but mention since you're paying me for my time."

"Meaning?"

"Meaning that you're the center of your life, Mister Frye. Everything you think about revolves around you."

"That isn't normal?"

"To a degree, as I said. But not to this degree."

"Meaning?"

"You have a bit of a narcissistic complex, Mister Frye."

"I think I pretty much knew that already, Doctor. My parents were delinquent and I was an only child. No one else to talk to during my childhood except for my friends at school."

"Yes, we'll get to that."

"What's that mean."

"Means that we'll get to that."

"When?"

"Not today."

"When?"

"Let's say next time."

"We have to meet again?"

"Several times, Mister Frye. Several times more."

"You must be rich, Doctor."

"Why?"

"All these appointments to tell me why I have nightmares."

"You'll thank me for it, Dylan. In the end we'll get to the root of your problems and you'll thank me for it. Really you will."

"I hope so. Doctor. Do I go now?"

"Yes, Mister Frye. That's it for today. It has been a pleasure to meet you. It really has."

But Dylan's nightmares increased, both in number and the fear they generated. Rather than helping, it seemed his choice of psychiatrists had made them worse.

"They're getting worse, Doctor."

"To be expected. They're fighting my attempts to weaken them."

"You talk as if they are separate from me."

"In a strange way they are, Mister Frye. Now let's get to it."

"What?"

"Tell me about them and, as you do, see if you can pinpoint anything particular in your waking life that might have initiated them."

So he did, several times and over several visits. Only thing that happened was that his daily life got as bad as his rare sleeping life. Finally, he'd had it and confronted the doctor.

"Listen, I'm paying you a fortune, Doctor, and nothing has helped, only made things worse. Not right. This doesn't work for me. Can you believe it? Ten visits and I'm worse now than I've ever been. I can't take much more of this."

"Good, Dylan."

"Good?"

"No, I mean it. Good in that you've reached the end of your tether. Really. No, I mean it. I really do. I told you they'd get worse before they got better."

"Yeah, but when are they going to get better?"

"Soon, Dylan, soon."

"Soon as in what, Doctor. Another year. Or today."

"Today, Dylan. Today. We're going to get you started on recovery today. This very day. Today I tell you. Right now if you want."

"Why did we wait this long?"

"I had to get to know you, Dyl. I really did. Trust me. Knowing you is the most important part. If I tried to fix your problem without knowing you, it would be a shot in the dark, you see. But knowing you as I do now. After our first year, I know you, right? No, I really do. Listen, I've seen a lot of people with the kinds of problems you have and, believe me, lots of them. Dozens of them. No, hundreds of them. No, really, I mean it. No one's complained yet. Not a single person, I tell you. A perfect record. You'll thank me, Dyl. You will. You'll thank me."

"Stop, Doctor. Stop. You're beginning to sound like me. What do I do?"

"Stop, Dylan, stop."

"But how do I do that, Doctor?"

"Stop. A lot of people ask me this, Dyl. You wouldn't believe how many. If I'm being honest, I mean, if I'm being honest, that's what you have to do. Really. It is. Only thing you have to do."

Dyl tried it. Didn't work, so he tried another psychiatrist. This time a woman psychiatrist. One who came with good credentials and boy did she have good credentials. A perfect pair, and a body to match. As much as he enjoyed their sessions together, he continued to get worse. So once again he asked around and found a third person, this time old as time itself and looking like he'd fall asleep at any moment. No, really. He immediately saw the wisdom of his ways. This guy was good, very, very good. He was Dylan's favorite by far, though not as much a looker as his last one was. That could be guaranteed.

"So, Mister, Mister, Mister . . ."

"Frye."

"Yeah, that's right. Mister Frye."

"Yeah?"

"Yeah what?"

"You said so, Doctor. I assumed that you were going to tell me something."

"Tell you what?"

"What's wrong with me."

"Something's wrong with you?"

"Yeah. I can't sleep because of the nightmares I have."

"Nightmares, huh? What kind of nightmares?"

"The kind that keep me awake most nights."

"That's not good."

"No, it isn't. What can I do about it?"

"About what?"

"The nightmares."

"They keeping you awake?"

"Yes."

"Stop having nightmares. Easy."

"But I don't know how."

"Don't know how what?"

"To stop having nightmares."

"Here. Take one of these before you go to bed at night. Put you out like a light and you couldn't dream a bad dream if your life depended on it."

"Pills."

"Yeah. You don't like pills?"

"I'd a lot rather know what's wrong with me."

"You don't know what's wrong with you?"

"No, I do. I have nightmares and am afraid to go to sleep."

"Okay. Take one of these and you'll sleep like a baby. No more nightmares."

"What if that doesn't work?"

"Take two of them."

"What?"

"Two of them. Two of them. What, you can't hear now? That your problem?"

But they did work. Dylan slept like a baby. His insurance paid for the pills. His third doctor had been the best. Take a pill, and better life through chemistry. A perfect solution. One visit and out.

He should've come to this doctor first not last. But, at least he'd found him. A walking pharmacist.

16. Pills And Hair

Dylan, now closing in on forty and making money by the barrel load, still had many problems. His looks, for one. He liked the ladies. Plenty. Especially the middle of his psychiatrists though she hadn't helped him much. Hadn't given him pills that had worked.

Dyl's biggest 'looks' problem, in *his* mind at least, was his hair. Not so much the wrong color or straight instead of curly, but his growing lack of it. Going bald and not by fits and starts but all at once. His father had been bald, from what he could remember, and was proud of it, but that made Dyl all the more aware of his own loss.

So, in what spare time he had, he browsed the various Big Apple shops that dealt with men's wigs, hairpieces, toupees, postiches, perukes, comb overs, and so on. He tried them on, looked at them in mirrors from every angle, compared their abilities to withstand high winds, swimming pools, showers, and thus and so, and decided, after so much of his time spent, that he would go for implants. Follicle by follicle implanted hair that would not grow but would not otherwise blow away, at least not immediately.

Thus, after a painful month of surgeries, in the sense of suffering a festering blister the size of a watermelon on the end of your nose, Dyl found himself once again looking like a younger man. Not in actual years spent on planet Earth, but in terms of his appearance to the ladies, and dating. Nothing turned a lady off more than a bald pate. Now he had hair that he could prove his own by any standard except watching it grow.

Then he set about to see his quite-a-pair second psychiatrist outside her office. He was a rich man, and though she certainly had money given her hourly rate, she couldn't compare her fortune to his by any means. Believe it or not she accepted his offer and they met for the first time at eight in a high-class restaurant in Manhattan, a place that was definitely not a joint.

Seated at their table within a minute of their arrival though the place was known for the difficulty of getting seating, Dyl decided to let her do most of the talking. It had worked before and should work again. He forgot, though, the nature of her profession. Would she make up for it by talking when eating or sit like a wooden puppet, asking brief questions and listening the whole time?

She talked, and talked, and talked some more. Like Alicia had on their first date so long ago now. Didn't matter to Dyl, though. She'd worn a dress with a décolletage to die for, and he spent his time guessing how long before he'd get a shot at massaging those babies with his lips.

They, or rather she, spoke of everything happening in the great city. From symphony concerts of which Dyl knew nothing so nodded like he did, to psychiatry of which he knew only about the chemistry involved. She was a Democrat, him a Republican, but he didn't care. There was nothing about her he didn't like. Nothing. He knew that she would be his second wife. So much different than Alicia, and so much bigger in every way. Even her name was at the other end of the alphabet, Samantha. Sam for short. What a great name for such a great lady. Samantha.

Dyl knew that she knew he was a real-estate tycoon, but that didn't faze her in the least. Thank God, though, she didn't give him time to talk, for she was a whiz, and he a numbskull in comparison. He'd need to bone up, ah, in so many ways, in order to keep up with her.

As they went from the main course to dessert, he discovered that her privacy according to the psychiatric rule she'd signed bound her to never reveal any patient's case but that she was quite able to tell stories out of class, so to speak. In other words, Sam could talk in general about the types of cases she'd worked on but not reveal a single name of any of her patients. This, of course, opened up a whole new area of soliloquy for her and kept her talking through dessert and on the way home, and entirely through the lovemaking process. While this unnerved Dyl a bit, he didn't care much. Found it sexy as a matter of fact, and it wasn't until she left the bed afterward leaving him in a stunned silence that he realized what he had. A genuine counterbalance for himself. No wading through details, enjoy and turn her off.

She told him his own story without realizing it, and that brought him to climax for some reason. A connection of some sort. No actual names, of course, that would have been unprofessional and litigable were it to come to that.

So, the new woman in his life, the one who listened to her patients the entire day, talked non-stop the rest of the time. Even in her sleep. Dyl wondered whether it was he or she that needed help. Taking his pills helped him sleep. Maybe she should take some as well.

But he loved Sam, the veritable woman of his dreams. A man's woman, or so he thought of her. If he got sick of listening, only thing he had to do was slip her a mickey by putting one of his pills in her drink and she'd be out like a light for the full duration of the night. What a dream. Of course, she barely knew what he did for a living, didn't care, but that was fine with him. She had real degrees and he didn't. Her vocabulary eclipsed his manifold. Her intelligence dwarfed his carburetor. No reason to be intimidated by having to talk.

So their relationship grew, her loving his ability to shut up and listen, and he loving her for, well, the obvious. Quickly, therefore, they spoke of marriage, pre-nuptial agreements that favored him, not her, and them writing their own vows with hers at least a ream larger than his, though Dyl's nothing more than a trifle full of the glories of his new wife's attributes, sans those the attendees to the wedding would discover quickly enough just by looking.

17. The Name

Dyl's first attempt at creating something rather than making money on what others created, came during his one-sided courtship with Samantha. He'd gotten the idea from others that he could contract a building with his own name on it that could serve many purposes, rentals and stores on the bottom floors, corporate offices on the middle floors, and luxury penthouses and sales on the top floors with the really great views. A forty-seven-story beauty that would, while not competing for New York City's tallest, could match, at least in some ways, the Big Apple's best.

He had the money for a large down payment, borrowed the rest, and hired and fired architects, planners, contractors, and so on, making it one hell of an original job and calling it the Frye Towers, right in the heart of the Fashion District. The perfect place for the best of the best, as he would call it.

Dylan had a field day ordering his staff around and hiring and firing as was necessary and sometimes for the fun of it. He'd mortgaged his business and given his saved fortune up for this baby, and he wasn't going to let any of it be less than the perfection he imagined his namesake deserved.

Along the way, though, maybe by not paying attention to the contracts he signed and the fact that once on board, many of his smarter staff had figured they might get the ax and so built in a full payment for services rendered regardless of their fulfilling those services due to the likelihood of being fired along the way. Whatever, Dylan rode the pony through to the end, on the last day watching at night as the four iterations of the Frye Towers' lights begin flashing in four directions, seen from anywhere in the greatest city on earth. His name. His dream. His nightmare.

Within the week, the various contractors and their minions came proverbially knocking at Dylan's door and within hours, not days, he knew he couldn't borrow enough to pay them back. Woefully short of funds and the enemy of everyone in the area, Dyl had no choice but to declare Chapter 7 bankruptcy, this being the one in which a debtor's non-exempt assets are sold via a trustee and the proceeds distributed to the creditors according to the priorities established in the relevant code for such. In other words, hard come, easy go. Retaining the name Frye Towers, his building, the one he'd built, was sold to pay those who labored in part or in full to build the thing.

So imbalanced was the cost of the 'towers' to the amount that Dyl could afford and borrow, that he suffered a complete collapse of everything he'd worked so hard to create. None of it was his any longer, even his business and the money going back as far as the gambling extortion from his high school days. Dylan had gone from the top of the mark to the bottom of the barrel in but a few days, maybe weeks, but it felt to him like days.

Yet he had three things going for him. His insatiable desire to succeed—meaning making lots of money and thus gaining power, the love of his life's stash of savings to live on, and an ego the size of

Manhattan. These personal attributes had worked before, and they would work again. No doubt in Dyl's mind about that and, were it known, little doubt in anyone who thought they knew him either.

Luckily, Frye Towers had paid off most of his encumbrances leaving him generally squared as he planned his next venture, this one a combination of two of his dreams, not one.

First, he dreamt of another building, this one wider and taller and more ambitious than the last. Second, this building was not in The City, but in another city of lesser size, that being Atlantic City in New Jersey where he likely wouldn't have to deal with those skeptical of him remaining solvent. Third, the make up of his dream building was a combination of two things he loved, gambling and himself. Interestingly, aside from his profession of gambling his entire fortune with every venture, he knew that raking in another fortune to cover any initial losses with the input from his casino would guarantee him not facing another bankruptcy. Mostly, though, it was the location. Near to where he lived, still in the mini-mansion where he'd grown up and which had been saved from the previous debacle by having been willed to him by his parents and having certain built-in guaranties that bankruptcy could not touch.

So, with nothing in the bank and a somewhat debauched reputation, Dylan Frye set out to raise the collateral to build a major new casino slash hotel near the boardwalk in Atlantic City, New Jersey, with a view of the sea to die for, and plush rooms that the clientele would adore. Of course, knowing the area as he did, he included a large parking garage. For this wasn't the city of cabs, but, more like LA, a city of cars.

Obviously, the first few potential lenders gave him the cold shoulder. But Dyl, ever the iconoclast, wasn't fazed in the least. In fact, he turned things on their head. Whenever he got the bad news, he spent the next weeks upping the grandeur of some aspect of the building and thus raising the price. He considered that the more the thing would cost to build, the more likely someone would invest in it.

Finally, though, he had to give up one of his dreams, the name. He'd wanted his on the marquee but realized that wouldn't be possible this time around. Mad that the new owners of the Frye Tower in The Big Apple had taken his name down and added theirs, he'd have to add this letdown to his others for the sake of being realistic.

A year passed as he spent his days pandering to those who had money, and listening to his wife-to-be patter on without him listening. One year stretched toward two, with glorious sex, inglorious lack of success, and him inheriting a dog named Gloria from a neighbor, something he hadn't planned on but had proven to be a major addition to his life. He'd take Gloria everywhere, a little poodle as cute as the day was long and a real charmer to those he peddled his new building to.

Almost two years to the day from when he'd made his decision, he found someone willing to take a chance, a multi-billionaire who sought something in his waning years to leave at least his name to posterity. A hotel-casino that would endear him forever to those who loved to make the big gamble that might take them from near homelessness to the riches they surely deserved.

After twenty-four months of hope, Dylan Frye was on his way again. Doing what he loved to do best, and living the beautiful life of eventual money, power, and, of course, love of his new wife-to-be who never, never stopped talking.

18. Tall Buildings

It took another two years to complete the building, but when finished, Dylan looked up at the grand structure, breathed a sigh of relief that once again he'd found the right track, and reeled in the money that he'd had enough foresight to take a percentage of from the gambling up front, for none of the actual tower was his, or even a fraction of the parking garage's income. But he'd spilt the casino's profits with the owner, the man who'd bankrolled the whole project and whose name emblazoned the top in blinking red, white, and blue lights that some said could be seen ten miles out at sea, and those proved significant enough for him to once again open his real-estate business.

As he did, Dyl popped the question to Sam and she accepted. He knew everything was well because as he did it, on bended knee no less, he felt a great relief overtake him. This was the one. Absolutely. He knew it in his bones. She would make him whole where Alicia had made him less than he was when unmarried.

Two months later, they tied the knot, this time in a private ceremony with no parents present—both sets dead from similar accidents—and but a few friends of each partner present to make it legal as in best man, bridesmaid, and so on, and a great time was had by everyone and once again Dylan could see the light of day at the end of his tunnel.

As was always the case with Dyl, though, something came up that dampened his spirits. This time, law suits. It seemed that his design of the hotel slash casino he'd built in Atlantic City roughly matched that of another casino in Las Vegas. Someone had noticed and suddenly he found himself facing court dates, subpoenas, affidavits, hearings, allegations, arbitrations, testimonies, summary processes, briefs, continuances, damages, depositions, *voir dires*, dockets, eminent domains, injunctions, and interrogatories, to name a few. Reminded him of his days as a gofer in law firm, memories he hated and hated more for being forced upon him by idiots like those suing him.

So he hired a lawyer, one that came with good bona fides and yet a lower than average fee. But it unfortunately kept him busy and away from Sam, his business, and from Gloria since dogs were not allowed in courtrooms, law offices, or prosecutors' offices. During this time, however, he had the good fortune of meeting a man named Tom Benchley, a lawyer who had a true gift for gab, something Dyl thought he'd cornered the market on, but realized he hadn't after meeting Tom.

After meeting Dyl, Tom got right to the point, "Aren't you the one who bankrupted on the building named after you in The City?"

"Lies," Dyl answered, "all lies. Never happened to us. Never. The whole thing, made up. Horrible lies, I tell you."

"Might work," Tom replied, "but I doubt it. Someone's going to look it up."

"You got a better idea?"

"Sure. Everything's positive. Like maybe, 'Sure it happens to everyone. Many times. Many, many times. Me, only once. To Frye it happens once and they make a big deal out of it. Once. Only once. Bankrupt me and it's a big deal. I'm working on a new building now in Atlantic City that will shame that one into nothing. People are coming to me now like they never did. Many people. Hundreds of people. We'll make the New York City fiasco into small potatoes, let me tell you.' How did you like that?"

"Not bad," Dylan said. "Positive, huh. Make everything positive."

"Not every thing, no, you have to have a little balance. Like ask me the same question, okay?"

"Sure. What was it now? 'Aren't you the one who bankrupted the building in The City?'"

"No. *They* bankrupted me. *They* did it. You ask around I did everything right. From the beginning."

"Short?"

"As short as possible. Keep most of it positive, and use 'we' more and 'love' a lot more, and talk about yourself in third person. Like, 'Frye loves you.' Things like that. Try it."

"About what?"

"How about the same stuff. Frye Tower."

"Okay. Listen, Frye Tower was the best we ever built, ask anybody. Really. It was such a great honor to build that building. Unbelievable. So we went over budget a little. No reason to push the panic button. But they did anyway. Babies. Every one of them babies. Gutless wonders."

"Not bad. You catch on fast. Negative, short and sweet, positive, keep dishing it out. Always."

They talked about other stuff in the same way. Tom became Dyl's lawyer of choice, not only because he got him off most of the time, but because he didn't work for a firm of two hundred other lawyers and a team on top that got paid outrageous bucks for doing absolutely nothing.

The most important thing that Tom taught Dylan was never accepting settlements on lawsuits. Hang tough and beat them. Lie, cheat, and buy witnesses if you have to, but never settle. Once you settle it's over. They peg you for that and know that they can get something for suing you for anything. Beat them into the ground a few times and the word will get out, don't bother Frye on a class action or you'll end up owing him money. Same goes for individuals. Never settle.

During this time, Dyl and Gloria got to know one another well. Best of friends. Man and dog. Unfortunately, Dyl got to know Sam but Sam didn't get to know Dyl. When Dylan came home from a rough day, Sam wouldn't let him get a word in edgewise. Always with the words, many of which he didn't understand, not that he listened that much. With a cook, housecleaner, and her not wanting babies because it would hurt her career, things slowly went south.

At first it didn't matter that much. He could stay at work some nights, sleeping on a couch generally reserved for clientele. Quickly, though, Dylan grew a bit anxious—or shall we say horny—for someone who would listen and at least pretend to enjoy their lovemaking. Thus it was that Dyl had the first affair of his life. No big deal for him. But, as it turned out, a very big deal for Sam when she discovered the extramarital relationship after a few months of sleeping alone too often.

She hired a private dick who took less than a day to get the photos. She paid him from her own salary and presented the pictures to Dyl the very same day. Dylan, of course, admitted to the thing immediately and attempted his best to say he'd been raped and that the thought that he'd cheat on his wife was as ridiculous as fizz in a good bottle of wine, and 'Dyl still loved her,' but unlike his lawyer's advice promised, she didn't buy a word of it and the next day papers were served.

Dylan tried to become despondent over the issue but couldn't get up for it. They'd not grown apart but never been together really in the first place. He'd loved her for her body from the first time he'd seen her and had to admit to himself that whatever he'd felt for her came about as a result of having to constantly remind himself that her talkative nature was something she'd outgrow. She hadn't, and thus, the divorce, decreed by their prenuptial agreements, was inevitable and meaningless in the long run. Maybe he wasn't cut out to be married. Not the marrying kind. He didn't really have anything for Mandy, his playmate on the side. Only something to relieve him of his busy life and from those physical pressures that most men feel, and woman, he supposed.

The new building that Dyl had constructed had run three billion in cost, without furnishings of any kind including the various costly items for the casino that took over the bottom floors. It looked it. Flashy as any found in Lost Wages for sure, and, to his mind at least, much more dignified and original as well. The investors added their name in the nice acronym 'GAMBOLS' and like the others blinked from the lights like the old Hollywoodland sign, first the whole thing, followed by each letter individually, and once again the whole thing. Wait five seconds, and the whole gizmo ran over again. Every day and every night, never stopping, even on Christmas.

Dyl never gambled, never drank liquor, no smoking, no drugs, no coffee, but he loved to watch others do these things, at least when it came to gambling. So he visited 'his' casino often, especially at night now that Sam was no longer around, leave Gloria with one of the doormen, and wandered. Every time someone rang up a one-armed bandit, he'd grin and count another probable increase in his cut of the profits. He loved the twirling, whirling, blinking, and winking lights on the machines, and the partially clad waitresses that wandered among the clientele to serve them drinks and cheese and crackers.

It was there that one night he laid his eyes on Katrina for the first time. Everyone called her 'K,' for short. Not Kay, but the single letter 'K' for some reason. A beautiful girl with blond hair and a body to die for, especially in that little costume she wore to impress the guests. When he got close to her to hear her speak, she had that German accent that sounded like the actress Hedy Lamarr. Looked like her a bit, too, and that said a lot given Hedy had often been called the most beautiful woman in the world. If love could happen at first sight, Dylan had caught the bug. His brash ability to come up to someone he didn't know and talk non-stop didn't work with Hedy, or K, didn't matter by what name he called her.

In fact, to meet her, he arranged to bump into her as she left the casino one night, him with Gloria to break the ice. Everyone thought Gloria was the cutest dog on earth, especially women, and K was definitely that. Bingo, ten minutes later, after watching K fondle Gloria and jealousy rear its head, he and she, K that is, had a date for dinner after she got off work for the next night.

Unlike Alicia with her penchant for profanity and Sam with her impossible love for talking nonstop, K was a perfect partner for Dylan. First, she respected his ability to speak so eloquently and to bravely go where no one else had gone. Second, she was demure in an old-school way. She loved to smile and bat her eyes in his direction. Third, and maybe most important, she had scruples, one of which involved not engaging in sex until she was married. Petting yes, real thing, no. She became an idol in his eyes and he couldn't keep himself away from her. Unlike Alicia and Sam, his love of her intensified with each date rather than the reverse. She was the real thing, he knew it and she knew it. So it was no surprise when he popped the question and a lesser surprise when she accepted. Maybe a little surprise when she convinced him they wait for six months to make sure their marriage would last.

Life was good for Dyl, and he knew it might never get better. Never could get better.

19. Casinos

It did become better though, as Dyl, needing to work to keep himself from going crazy during the times he couldn't be with Hedy, or K as was her name, he stumbled onto the biggest opportunity, the biggest deal of his life.

A major player on the Las Vegas strip approached Dylan with the deal to end all deals, building a major casino in the city of casinos that would take the area by surprise. A European style gambling palace like the Europeans built. A place of places. A miracle in the desert. Something that looking at the skyline would immediately jump out and grab your attention. A perfect fake of what would normally appear in Monaco but never in Nevada in the U.S. of A. The building of buildings.

As he listened, Dyl couldn't believe his ears. This place would have everything—ballrooms, convention centers, shows to end competition, big bands from the fifties, great stars, restaurants to die for, rooms of Greek design with sunken hot springs in the living area, one-hundred inch television sets with Internet access, Roman columns everywhere, naked ladies dancing and whatever else naked ladies did in places like this in Vegas, and the highest building in Lost Wages with the largest footprint in the sand. His, of course, blinking like a Christmas tree in full view of every airplane landing and taking off from the city of faux everything. Five years in the making, but a guaranteed winner in every way. The deal of a lifetime, no question about it. The only thing Dyl had to do was to say yes.

Of course, Dyl wouldn't own it exactly, but his name would grace its tallest tower since that name was associated, apparently and according to this guy, with fakery everywhere in the world. Nothing but compliments from this guy. Dyl loved it. He loved the guy, the deal, the building, the architect of the building, the whole ball of wax. Vegas was the king of crap, and who better to deal with crap but the master himself. Away from the east coast and into the city where nothing was real but the money. As long as you could hold onto it.

Though, was it too good to be true? He'd never dealt with the likes of the man who'd come to him bearing such gifts. Gracious beyond belief. Completely open about his proposal and in that, no fine print or qualifiers. But five years? He'd have to move his base of operations to Nevada and what about K? Traveling nearly coast to coast every few days would cost him half his commission.

The 'deal' went like this. Dylan would oversee construction from the largest metal strut to the minutest detailed plastic flower in a guest room for a high six-figure yearly salary for five years with, depending on his evaluation at the end of each year, expectation of a fifteen percent raise leading to a million-dollar final year. His name would appear as the name of the place and he could live there anytime he wished free of charge for the rest of his life.

How could he refuse, especially with nothing else on his plate at the moment. Everything except K was perfect. He'd have to work that detail out. A rider on the contract allowing him and a significant other to live free of charge for five years in a competing hotel in Vegas to allow him continual access to the construction site.

Fine, the man told him and guaranteed the revised contract would arrive that afternoon for his signature.

What could go wrong? How, indeed, could anything go wrong?

With negotiations wrapped up in a week's time and with Dyl's best lawyer having gone over every detail to his satisfaction, Dylan signed the necessary papers and proceeded to ask K to marry him, something she agreed to within seconds, and he moved his world lock stock and barrel west to the land of fantasy and riches, at least for him. The only things he kept were his mini-mansion in Jersey and his dog Gloria.

His first year went swimmingly well. His Austrian-born wife Katrina loved everything about Vegas except the summer heat, Gloria loved everything about Katrina and, of course, Dylan, and Dyl loved his job. No kibitzers, lots of illegal immigrants who worked for next to nothing, and thus, he came in well under budget for his first year and on target for completion in four more. He got his raise and everything looked good to better than good. A perfect match on every count.

That is, until the B word re-entered the world of Dylan and his now growing family—K's first baby of many to come arriving within days of the bad news. It seems that the backers of the deal he'd made had grossly overestimated what they could raise during the first year, that or they never intended to raise it in the first place hoping to sue Dylan for incompetence and threatening to force the city to complete the job to avoid the eyesore of the first twenty floors half completed and with the scaffolding still standing for the next twenty floors for everyone to see out their airplane windows as they approached the city of their dreams, a Disneyland for adults. What these backers received in return for bankruptcy and losing their stake in the project, was the notoriety of having planned the building, the best in LV, and the architect's plans eventually completed since the lower-floor design dictated the precise construction based on the blueprints. In other words, the city, county, or whomever the judge dictated would carry on with the project, had to follow the plans generated by the original team. Either that, or themselves keep the funding going to finish the project with Dyl and the original backers still in charge, immediately paying back and forward salaries and ending up with four-fifths of one of the city's greatest landmarks, a solution that the city council ultimately chose.

All these machinations more than confused Dyl, but Tom's clever hands in the various pots worked it out in a way that every 'I' got dotted and 'T' got crossed to ensure that Dyl's good name was cleared and basically everyone but the city father's came out smelling like roses. The city raised its taxes on the casinos in general to make up the difference and only the new Frye Casino and Hotel, notice the order of those words, came out on the long end of the stick. Smelling like roses, as they say.

Of course, this description makes everything appear easy. It wasn't. Dyl's first year of marriage was tough on both him and K, and his life was hell, basically having him both deal with his coming family, build the building, and spend time in court talking his way out of every manner of this's and that's that someone or other claimed he'd done, from being part and parcel of the plot to hiring those illegal immigrants and paying them one-tenth of union wages.

"You claiming you paid those indigents a proper wage, Mister Frye?"

"No, Your Honor, I'm *stating* that they got what they're worth."

Your Honor was not happy with that answer but he'd heard worse from Mister Frye and had heard rumors of much worse from others in the rumor mill and, given the tenacity of Tom Benchley, took him at his word, whatever that meant.

"How did work go today dear?" K asked him one day.

"Long, love," he replied and fell immediately asleep at the table, head down in his folded arms.

And on and on, life getting more complicated by the moment.

20. Loving To Be Loved

When the building finally stood upright and the rooms outfitted with their proper equipment and furniture, Dyl fell asleep staring at his baby from inside the airport terminal in a seat designed for passengers to occupy rather than real-estate capitalists. But no one bothered him as he snored his way into a pill-less night of guiltless and nightmare-less bliss.

Since no one knew where he was at the moment, he slept through his and K's second child's birth, leaving both wife and newborn missing his presence and joy. But K understood, a perfect example of the famed European grace and humility, or maybe Katrina's version of such, and the next day everything was well as he brought mother and daughter Katherine—yes with a K—home to their hotel room and readied them for a move to their new haunts as promised, their free suite at the new Frye Casino and Hotel as promised by his original contract.

Thus began the two Dylan Fryes, the one that loved to be loved by those who said or often screamed that they loved him and to love those who loved him or at least screamed that they loved him. This version of Dyl smiled, stuck out his hand—left or right didn't matter—with a thumbs-up signature for victory. He waved at people in crowds as if he knew them but really didn't, and often crowed that "we love you," without much explanation as to who 'we' were. The second Dylan Frye at least pretended he didn't care but really did care. This version involved him saying things like, 'Horrible lies,' 'Getting even,' 'She hates me,' and 'Ever see him in person? A mess, I tell you,' and more things along those lines.

Having two personalities is not a new thing, in fact many psychiatrists will tell you everyone has at least two, and have names for them as in 'ego and 'alter-ego.' But no one most psychiatrists had ever seen could switch from one version to another in such record speeds. Frye could do it several times a minute depending on the situation. Interviews, which he found himself giving more and more since his new Vegas building was completed, provided the most evidence of such switches.

"So, so and so tells me that he thinks you're the best at what you do ever. You, Mister Frye."

"Well, he would know. He's the best. We love him. Honestly, he's the greatest. You know I've known him forever. Forever. The guy's been wonderful to me and my family and I love him. Greatest guy you'll ever meet."

"But another so and so told me he thinks you're full of hot air."

"Well, he would, I tell you. You know he tells such horrible lies. Can you believe it? The guy will never learn. Never. Absolutely never. It's unbelievable. I've tried to get him to think straight, but he won't. Unbelievable. Tell him for me when you see him next that he should listen to me. Listen for once rather than talking, talking, and talking. Can't get a word in edgewise. His own worst enemy. Worst enemy. Not me, but him. It's a shame, it really is."

Part of this negative aspect of Dylan Frye was 'getting even.' Not with words, but with actions. Beating the person at something. Maybe build it bigger or winning a game or getting the deal the other one wanted, and so on. He had words for getting even. He called them 'getting even.' But only to himself. Rarely did K hear him whisper the unmagical words to himself. He just did it. Didn't matter how long it took, grudges didn't have fuses attached, but he'd remember like an elephant supposedly did. Getting even, the version of the second Dylan Frye that no one, not his worst enemy, ever wanted to see.

Those in Frye's inner circle, if it could be called that, learned three things about him. His two versions was one. 'Getting even' was two. Third, and maybe the most critical of the three, was the inevitable volatility, usually centering around anyone, absolutely anyone, attempting to tell the man what to do. He was in charge of that, and he only.

Thus, approaching fifty now, *The* Dylan Frye, aside from his three personality traits, revolved around one thing and one thing only, and that one thing was Dylan Frye. His way or the highway. His dream or no dream. But watch out, his way, volatility, could turn on a dime and those caught in the crossfire would definitely feel the fanned flames of his direst moods.

21. Interviews

Living once again in the mini-mansion that his long dead parents had willed him, Dyl and his beautiful third wife and now three children, suffered the New Jersey winters and the east coast views of the Atlantic as Dylan continued to build his name value and claim accomplishments that many said but could not prove were nothing but hot air. He plied his real-estate trade with building casinos followed by bigger ones as his credentials grew, and far sooner than later his legacy accrued and his fortune blossomed into its former self. Say anything about him you wanted and it probably had or would happen, but claim the man didn't know the world of business and you'd be wrong. At least that's what he said about himself. For those in the know knew that it had been an up and down journey for Dyl and something most of his competitors had adroitly avoided. But Dyl arrived, and for that no one could argue.

Because of his ability to smile gracefully and grimace in apparent embarrassment of others not him, he found himself the target of interviews by the press. Any type of press. Television, radio, videos, newspapers, magazines, Internet, and many other media loved him, for no faster than the conversation began than Dyl would say something impossible for anyone to imagine and the editorials and pundits would crowd around for more, more, and more more. He had a way of attracting attention better than anyone else including the most out-there film stars. Want a good sound bite? Interview Frye. The best thing going. Better was the fact that Dylan denied saying something when the interviewer had it on tape and played it back for him and his audience, and Dylan, without a blink of an eye, explained that it had been taken out of a larger context or that the interviewer didn't understand a joke when he or she heard one.

When things got sticky, Dyl tended to either blush or fill up time with gobbledygook. This made interviewers angry, interruptive, and negative, asking harder and more embarrassing questions than they would have. Tom Benchly once again came to the rescue.

"Interviews? Short answers. A sentence or two at most and stating your opinion. Speeches, the opposite. Know your audience and pander to what they want. Simple."

Tom acting as interviewer: "So, Mister Frye, it's clear that you like to boast that you're a great businessman. Why do you do this when you've faced two bankruptcies during your career?"

Dyl: "Didn't face them, others did. Neither my fault. Check the records for yourself and you'll see that I'm telling the truth."

Tom: "Still too long. 'Didn't face them, others did. Neither my fault.' That's what you need. Remember, short answers puts the interviewer back on his heels. Makes them look for a follow-up question regarding your answer or give it up and go on to the next subject. Either of which puts you on the offensive. See my point. You always need to be in charge."

Tom as interviewer: "Mister Frye, you've lost fortunes in your business dealings and yet you claim to be rich."

Dyl: "Amazing isn't it? Amazing."

Tom: "One sentence, not two."

Tom as interviewer: "You claim to be an honest man and yet you've had affairs when married and often hire illegal aliens and non-union scabs that will work at half the pay."

Dyl: "Rumors spread by my competitors."

Tom: "Now you're getting the idea. Keep it simple and direct. Always. I felt like you were in charge of the interview rather than me."

"What if they're really prepared?"

"Ask them to research something they haven't researched. Put them on their heels, Dyl, back on their heels."

Tom as interviewer: "We have it on good authority that you hire illegal aliens for constructing your buildings."

Dyl: "On what authority?"

Tom: "Too broad. Narrow it."

Dyl: "Have your authority meet my legal team and we'll see I'm right."

Tom: "Good. Now the opposite. Pretend you're speaking to the Rotary Club about, say, your basic principles."

Dyl: "I have to say that a lot of people have been asking me questions about this very subject. No, really, they have. A lot of people come up to me and ask if I still believe what I said. I tell them I always mean what I say. Always. Never doubt it. Look, if you want to get anywhere in this world you have to tell the truth and nothing but the truth, right? That's what I do. You know what I mean? I'm sure that you do the same. It's the right way to run a business and a right way to run a life. So, if I'm being honest, I mean really honest, as I am now I assure you, then you can always count on me for the correct answer. You never look back and wonder what I said. You never contradict yourself. The truth will set you free. I've always believed that and always will. I love that question, I really do. I love you for asking it. We love you. Completely love you. No one is better at telling the truth than me, and, of course you."

Tom: "Okay, I guess, but let's consider you're in a group of reporters, not only one so it's not an interview per se, but an interview nonetheless in a way. Try answering, 'How rich are you?' as if someone in a large group with you on stage asked it."

Dyl: Well, first, my fortune is fluid, you understand. It's probably gone up several notches since you last asked me that question. Believe me, I'd like to give you an answer but it would be different now than yesterday. Check the stock market, my bank's records, every one of those things and you'll see what I mean. I . . ."

Tom: "Wrong. This, too, is an interview. Shorter is better."

Dyl: "Too fluid to know at the moment."

Tom: "Better. How can they ask a follow up question to that? Fluid means changing and if it's changing, about the only thing they could ask would be 'Give me a rough round number?'" What would you say to that?"

Dyl: "Have many irons in the fire, could be something big that's changed."

"Perfect. Answers should at least imply that you're interviewing them. See my point?"

"Absolutely, Tom. You're a genius."

"You are right, Dyl. Absolutely right."

22. Empire

As his education by Tom progressed, so did Dyl's fortune, or imagined fortune that was pretty much the same thing in Dylan's mind. But no amount of money was enough for the growing Frye empire. He'd made the name 'Frye' a property, something one could invest in with secure knowledge that whatever occurred within that property, it would eventually pay off.

Thus, the Frye Radio Network came into being, at first a forum for Dyl to provide his brand of bull for anyone listening, the rest of the programming being canned stuff paid for with ads from companies believing in the Frye brand. Eventually, though, it became a network of several stations around the country broadcasting Dylan's dreams and ideas about the world's businesses, and how to work out deals to progress from small to big deals.

His favorite pastime grew quickly into a three-hour primetime call-in show where Dyl answered questions about how to become a billionaire. Mostly he lied or quoted Tom's views of such things, but the thing that worked best in the growing audience's numbers, was his volatility with callers. He might answer one with a curt, "Go look it up," and another with a, "We love that question," and rant on until the next commercial break before stopping.

Strangely enough, this particular show, called "The Truth," went national through a major radio network and spelled the immediate demise of his own network for which he worked for free. Now he worked for high seven figures and paid vacations. If he hadn't been rich prior to this amazing turn of events, he was now.

Dyl considered "The Truth" fun, not work. He looked forward to it. Especially on those days when the lines didn't light up and he had to hoof it by beginning with an off the cuff statement so outrageous that within seconds all sixty six lines lit up at once with a large group waiting in the wings.

"Fry the terrorists," he'd say for example, "Line them up and spray them with napalm." Half the country was listening with baited breath as callers attempted without success to change his mind or to join as soon as possible Dyl's army of enlistees that he said would someday take to the skies with the 'sweet smell of H-Bombs.' No one could top him. Want an audience, grab a Dylan hand grenade and pull the plug. Only one per customer, but only one necessary.

Funny thing was that it worked because he'd almost always put his finger on what everyone, left or right but not center, was thinking whether they would admit it or not. The more outrageous his thought was, the bigger and better the audience. More outrageous was that this same audience was not like those far right or far left dummies, it was everyone except those few not falling for his provocations.

Knowing his name was now second to none in visibility and recognition. He developed products to sell. Frye wine, for example. Frye newsletters, Frye investment hints, Frye websites guaranteeing products for a fee, a short-lived but interesting Frye film company, Frye on-line education with degrees offered for a price, Frye YouTube videos you could watch if you could endure the ads at the beginnings, Frye book reviews, Frye this, Frye that, Frye the other thing. It got so confusing that he had to hire people to handle the business many of them succeeded in bringing in. Most, of course, went slowly belly up given that people joined to see and hear Dyl not only to eat, drink, read, buy, see, and so on, products often without the name brand on them. But enough worked to give Dylan yet another way to make money and increase his power. And, of course, to spread his love for everyone who didn't hate his guts.

He joined the late night television comedic circuit, enjoying his ability to not answer questions he didn't like, instead giving the audience a Jack Benny eyebrow wiggle, or a roll of his eyes, or an exasperated grimace with his lips. Always, of course, with short answers, quips, and an occasional insult to keep things lively. Audiences looked forward to his guesting and loved his act, which is what it truly was. An act, I tell you. No, I mean it.

Slowly but surely, Dylan became an icon both in America and across the pond. No one could ever tell when he was joking or serious. Sometimes they found him both at the same time. He traveled as a showman might. He missed his family, but the dough rolled in and he reveled in the attention. Nearly as good as power, money, and love. Or maybe it was all three. What was not to like?

23. P. T. Barnum

Say what you might about Dylan Frye the real-estate tycoon, raconteur, and entertainer, he did spend quality time with his family when his schedule permitted, and was always more interested in them than himself, something many found hard to believe. Daddy was plain Daddy no matter his visibility to the world, and that was fine with him. Katrina, K, would agree with that when the occasional camera and interviewer turned her way for verification. There were more than two versions of Dylan Frye when the situation demanded it.

But, as time passed and as children are wont to do. Dyl's children grew into first their teens and followed by adulthood, leaving Dylan and Katrina alone in their mini-mansion or one of his hotel slash casinos across the country. With this time Dyl having found 'the one,' he relished these latter years as well as the former ones.

Now gaining ground on sixty years of age, the truly mature version of Dylan Frye blossomed into the P.T. Barnum he was destined to be with Phineas Taylor no doubt proud of his imitation self if he'd still been around. A true American showman, celebrated businessman, and part-time clown, Dylan continued to gain notoriety and profits from his various enterprises landing him the list of top-most wealthy men in the country and one capable of the most celebrated quotes of the new century. Like, "Learning from lost battles can win you the war," and "Give me a good piece of ass and I'll take it over anybody's damn opinion," and "You have bad breath," and "Winning's the most important thing, beats losing by a mile," and "It's always the right time to make a great deal," and "Shakespeare was right, readiness is everything," and "Never beat around the bush," and "Being rich, let me tell you, is better than being poor." So often was he quoted that when his last child left home for parts unknown, Dyl wrote a book that, when he discovered he really didn't know how to write a book or what to write about, he decided two things, that he'd have someone else write it, and that it would be about Dyl himself.

He titled his book "No kidding" and the man who wrote it tape recorded Dylan for a couple of weeks, had it transcribed, recombined the various sentences into an order that made sense, and *voila*, a book. A best seller, no less, and more money for the Frye coffers. There was nothing, apparently, that Dylan could not do. Having money was the best thing going.

One day, Dylan found himself bored, truly bored. Bored of people loving him for what he said, bored of people hating him for the same reason, and bored of making money by sitting around and twiddling his thumbs. Years and years of doing the same things had become truly boring, and he had to do something to change that. Every bit of that. No, I mean it.

So, Dyl visited his lawyer and mentor Tom Benchley for advice, and got it. Advice, I mean. Tom told him that Dyl ought to take the wonderful things he'd learned over the years and apply them to something that would get him something else in life that he'd always wanted. Something as different from what he was currently doing, but not so different that he could use his wealth of experience and knowledge to make a real go of it.

Dyl, of course, had never considered such a thing. What, for instance, did he want that he couldn't already buy? What did he want that he didn't already have or get if he wanted it bad enough? What does anyone want when they climb into their sixties and not already have?

Without further thought, he knew the answer to his questions. Power! He had money. He had love. But power? No way did he have enough of it. No way. So he gave that some thought. What would bring him more power than he already had?

When Dyl visited Tom with his question, Tom had an answer ready for him, not that he could read minds, but that he'd been preparing for such a question for weeks before it came.

Answer? Run for office. Any office, didn't matter, but likely one that wouldn't have a glass ceiling, one that would have a road to the highest levels. For as much as he, like others, had rebuked Dyl for some of his outlandish statements, most made sense when you gave them serious thought.

But he hadn't guessed that Dylan, if he'd come with a question, had already created an answer. He didn't wish to crawl up the ladder to the top, he wanted to start at the top.

Perfect Dylan.

"Run for President," he responded to Tom's suggestion. "Haven't the patience to take the long road there. Or the time, for that matter. Go right for the jugular like he'd gone for everything else in his life. Certainly no one would give him a chance. Didn't matter. Dylan Frye made his own chances. Simple as that. With this said, Benchley became the man behind the man, the one who would advise Dylan of the knocks to take and the ones to not take.

The very next morning, without giving the nod to his wife, Dylan Frye announced his candidacy on his morning radio show and prepared for that afternoon's combined press conference and forum with the people, his first campaign speech for his run to become the next President of the United States. No dallying around.

Straight to the top.

24. True Politics

Dyl knew his first foray into the world of politics would not begin with a bang, so he had Tom set it up by paying ringers to attend, to applaud his every word wildly, and to bring quickly printed signs indicating their absolute devotion to the man of the hour. The paint had just dried on those signs when the unprepared press and the barely prepared rented not press, shouted for joy when Dyl made his first appearance as a full-fledged candidate for the office of President of these United States.

The cameras rolled, the people standing supposedly in honor of the great man but in truth because no one had thought to bring and set up chairs to sit on, and the piped-in music played classical marches to suggest that outside the lonely doors stood a massive group of well wishers that weren't allowed inside because the fire marshals had been so stingy in allowing only the legal number of guests to enter and enjoy this milestone in American History. Of course, no one stood outside, for truth be known no one had the slightest idea what was going on inside those doors.

"C'mon in," shouted Dylan when set up with microphone and podium toward those invisible people, gesturing with his hands as he said, "hundreds of people here today to wish us the best in our reach toward the White House. Thousands of people. I love it. I love you people who could get in. Lucky people you are. We truly love you. It's a memorable day, let me tell you. A memorable day. Memorable. I'll be telling you why in a few moments. I know, I know, you can't wait. I love it. I absolutely love it. Love it. Truly. Such love in this place, I tell you. Truly there is. Love. Both ways, that's for sure. C'mon in. The fire marshals are gone. So many people. Thousands of people. I love it."

While Dyl adjusted the microphone in front of him, what there was of an audience, noting its cue, applauded vigorously.

"What a day, I tell you. You wouldn't believe it. When they heard I was running, they went nuts. What joy. I was completely thrilled. Some woman I saw gave me some money. I tried to give it back but she was gone before I could give it back. Such love, I tell you. Everyone. Everywhere. What a day."

Another microphone twitch and another round of applause, this time because it was the second such motion. People yelled and screamed and the group chanted the phrase, "We want Frye, We want Frye, We want Frye." Dylan smiled at them benevolently, like a king might his subjects, or an emperor his slaves. "Who knew it would be like this?" Dylan responded. "I mean, who knew? So much love. What a day. What a great day. I mean it. What a day."

As the cheering continued, Dyl took a long stroll around the stage, shaking hands with people he didn't know, waved and smiled to people he didn't know as if he did know them, and giving a soon-to-be famous wink to other people he didn't know. It wasn't long before the sham got lost and Dyl began to believe his own hype. Hard not to do given the wild enthusiasm that captured the entire hall. Even the cameramen, making their livings, were caught up in the rush of energy. Some of the press, the ones without cameras, had already left, but the ones with cameras, particularly the ones behind and running those cameras, added to the emotional frenzy that Dylan now understood that in some ways was real.

"Thank you," Dylan said as he signaled the audience again with his touch of the mic, "I can't tell you how much your appreciation means to me, and I won't let you down. Believe me when I say that. Believe me."

A microphone touch and another powerful rush of applause that this time took longer to quiet down.

"So I'll get right to it. You've probably heard rumors that I'm going to announce my candidacy for the Presidency of these United States of America."

Touch of the mic and more applause, this time uncontrollable.

Dylan looked at the few press remaining and at the cameras that no doubt had the talking heads back in the studios buzzing about his words and said, "It's true. I am announcing my candidacy for the Presidency of these United States of America."

Without touching the mic this time, everyone in the place jumped up and down, waved their now fully dried signs, and screamed their bloody heads off. No way was Dylan going to be able to stop this. No way. He'd have to wait it out. By now, though, he believed so strongly that his fakery was real, that if Almighty God had entered the room at that moment, He would have believed it as well, and, no doubt, blessed Dyl's campaign four times over given the love that he'd engendered with these people.

When it did die down, however, and Dyl had, once or twice, beckoned non-existent people outside the doors to come in and join them, he wound up his mental pitching arm and rode a fastball dead center to what the crowd wanted.

"Here's what we're going to do when I'm elected," he said, and the crowd screamed as if that had already happened and the first day of his first term of many had come about magically. "We're going to build a wall," he said, "that will extend along the entirety of the southern borders between us and the country of Mexico. A tall wall that no one can climb. One with razor wire on top so that if anyone tried to climb it they'd accomplish nothing but tangling themselves up and hanging from it the rest of their lives. Imagine that many Mexicans dangling from the top of the wall, bleeding themselves out, and never getting to see the great lands of our country. The addicts, dealers, gangs, prostitutes, homeless, murderers, rapists, and you name it will hang there for eternity with nothing but their dried bones to show for it. What a sight, huh? I mean what a sight. You know what will make this worth its weight in gold? They'll pay for it. Every one of those bastards. They'll pay for the wall. They will. How, you ask. Because I'll make them pay, that's how. Trust me. I know how to do that and I will. You've read my books and you know I will. We're tired of the pussies in Washington, I tell you. We're, you and me, going to take back our country. That's the freedom cry of our movement I tell you. 'Take back our country.' Soon you'll see hats and jackets, and signs, and T-shirts, and car and truck bumpers with that on them. 'Take back our country,' they'll say, and mean it. We're going to fix our country, not spend every hard-earned buck on the rest of the world. No, I mean it. We're going to take back our country. Take back our country, I tell you. That's our motto. Say it with me."

"Take back our country."

"Take back our country."

"Take back our country."

"Take back our country."

The room started to rock with the sound, as if a giant was stomping the ground outside and shaking the building they inhabited.

"Incredible," Dyl said above the din. "Absolutely incredible."

"Take back our country."

"Take back our country."

"No, I mean it, you're incredible." And, one by one, the people paid to do this got really caught up in the mob rule of the place.

"I love you," Dyl screamed. "We love you. We really do." At that moment, just for that moment, Dyl really *did* love them, and them him. No more P.T. Barnum. The real thing. Dylan Frye and his people. Loving each other. The networks, cable, and the Internet grooved with the sound of "Take back our country." They believed it, too. Who wouldn't? This was a moment in history where rules didn't apply, at least rules not governed by the chemistry inherent in the human body. For Dylan Frye had stirred something that would take sometime to unstir. He'd drummed up a fundamental urge in the human psyche that would take some time to undo.

"Take back our country."

25. Take Back Our country

Dyl rode that horse all the way to the stables that afternoon. He punched buttons, waved magic wands, and hit every sensitive nerve he could. He used his Wall to keep out terrorists, trade agreements, foreign wars, thus giving us more money to spend on our infrastructure, and dozens, no hundreds, maybe thousands of other things that we hated. Every one of them that thought seriously about such things. That meant everyone in the room and those watching on television.

When he'd finished his first stump speech, Dyl came off stage and found Tom Benchley waiting for him.

"Not bad," Tom said.

"Not bad? What're you talking about? Did you see those people out there? Mad about me. They loved me. We love them. It was a love fest."

"Remember, Dyl, we paid them to love you. Next time we won't pay them."

"But I did good, didn't I?"

"Sure you did. But we've got to prepare for next time."

"So quick?"

"Right now."

"Now? Can't we take a break?"

"No. We've got to run with what we've got right now."

"All right. But how?"

"You ever play chess, Dyl?"

"Sure, I guess. When I was in my teens a bit."

"Remember how the pieces move?"

"Sure."

"The point of the game? I mean 'checkmate?'"

"Yeah."

"Well think now, right now, about checkmate."

"Okay."

"All right. Your opponent tips his king over and that's it, right?"

"Yeah."

"How do you get that to happen?"

"You mean how do I win the election?"

"Precisely."

"How do I do that at this point? Don't know who my opponents are."

"You will, though, faster than you wish. But regardless, you've got to keep your eye on the goal, not the skirmish that will inevitably bubble up occasionally, or in your case, often. Everything you do from your first move is going to affect the outcome of the game, right?"

"Yes."

"Okay, we keep that goal not only in mind from the beginning, we keep our plans for mate in mind from that point on. Get that?"

"Sure. But how? Too many things can happen between now and then."

"Right. But without the overall plan, or a plan that has to undergo occasional tweaks, you wander around hoping for the best. We're not going to hope, Dyl, we're going to win. Get it?"

"Fine. So what do we do?"

"We're not going to let the changes in the wind govern your plan, we're going to change the changes in the wind. Power, Dyl, power. We're in charge. Now, let me give you an example."

"Can we go somewhere where we won't be overheard?"

"Doesn't really matter, but okay, let's do that."

"What do you mean it doesn't really matter?"

"Doesn't really matter because they can't stop you even if they know what you're doing."

"Sounds better and better."

Once alone in the green room off the stage, Tom sat Dyl down and Tom explained it to him.

"Most people think that great chess players think ahead two or three moves when playing to win."

"Yeah."

"No. From the start of the game they plan the endgame. Got it. They look at the board with the pieces in place and decide how the board will look when their opponents tip over their kings in defeat. They more or less play the game backward to the beginning to see what they should do next."

"Isn't that impossible?"

"Probably on a move by move, position by position, process, yes. But not like pushing your opponents in certain general directions. Say, for example, if your point is to checkmate in the far right corner, you can generally make it impossible for your opponent not to give way to your power to guide him that way. See what I mean? While they're attempting to win pieces, battles shall we say, your idea is to move the game to your long-term advantage. Maybe gambit a little along the way. Give him pieces that makes him think he's winning the war when he's actually losing that war to your overpowering push toward your initial checkmate design."

"I get it."

"Do you?"

"Yes. It isn't so much what happens today but what happens in the distant future."

"Wrong. It does matter what happens today because everything you're doing is making that future you have in mind a reality. See, the point is to win the game, get the votes, not to show off what you can do that most likely won't help you achieve your goal. Making that crowd cheer isn't the plan, Dyl. It's nice. It made people today sit up and take notice all right, but you should never be happy unless what you did that day furthers you toward that eventual goal. Watching your opponent tip over their kings. Got it?"

"I think I do. Shouldn't take anything too seriously. Should make each and every thing I do work toward powering me to victory."

"Now you've got it. The only thing that counts is winning. Everything else, no matter how crazy it might sound or how dismal it might make you feel for the moment, if it gets you a victory at the end of the game, it's the perfect thing to do. So don't get too wired up about this or that. We plan our strategy carefully and keep our eyes on how we can incrementally take steps to achieve it. Could be that one day everyone will seem to hate you. Call you names. Doesn't matter it that's part of the plan. If its part of the plan you celebrate and make them hate you more. Without the winning plan, nothing works and you get flushed down the john, Dyl. Right down the toilet."

"Terrible metaphor, Tom, but I get the picture."

"Well, get used to it, Dyl, because today we set the plan in motion. You're on the way to the White House. Guaranteed. A done deal. If, that is, you keep your eyes on that prize, and nothing but that prize. We do what we plan to do. Right?"

"Right."

"Say it again."

"Right."

"Louder!"

"Right!"

Of course, Tom Benchley was right. As usual. The reaction in the press was mixed at best. Ugly at times, but front page in every paper.

"Frye talks." one headline read.

"Promises, Promises, Promises," said another.

"Millionaire Racist Declares Candidacy," ran yet another. This one, of course, made Dyl cringe.

"How does this help us?" he asked Tom when he saw him next, showing him the left wing paper's front page.

"Made people read it," Tom said. "First element of our plan, Dylan. We need to not only get everyone's attention, we need to charge their emotions into gear."

"But I'm not a racist."

"No, but at this point in the game you're an isolationist. To these guys it's the same thing. But you won't fire back. Think of it. Your opponents, of which there will be many, don't have their name in those headlines. Yours is. No one's reading about them today. They are reading about you. Negative, positive, doesn't matter at this early point in the process. Attention is what matters. Your name talked about, written about, watched on TV, worried about, and on and on. We'll change the rhetoric when the time comes and you'll love it."

"I guess," Dyl said, meekly.

"You'll see. Wait until tomorrow when you give your first real stump. We won't be paying anyone to show up, believe me, and those crowds outside the building that weren't there today? They'll be there tomorrow, and when you say thousands of people, you won't be lying. They'll be thousands. Maybe tens of thousands. Remember, at this point in the game you've done nothing but move a pawn to rook three. That's nuts and your opponent knows it. But he doesn't trust you so he's wary. Off his game already. See what I'm saying here?"

"Yes," Dyl said. "I do."

But he didn't have to like it.

26. The Press

Dyl began his speech the next day by dragging the press through the mud he'd created in his declaration of candidacy proclamation.

"The media, aren't they something though? I say I want to build a wall to keep illegal aliens out of the country. Not legal ones, mind you, but illegal ones. What do they not understand by the word illegal? So, what do they do? Call me a racist. Of course there are some good newspapers and pundits in this world. Many of them. They're fine. But these other guys, the one's calling me a racist, unbelievable. Truly unbelievable. They got nothing else to do with their time but call me names?"

The crowd went mad, yelling, screaming, and hoisting their signs that read, "Take back our country," provided conveniently by the management at no cost.

Dyl pointed at one of the cameras focused on him. "Where do you stand up there? No you, the guy behind that camera." The crowd booed without being coerced to do so.

"Don't boo him. Maybe he's one of us. Are you?"

Without thinking, except maybe about his life coming to an end, the cameraman nodded, and with him the camera itself. Up and down. Up and down. "Don't worry folks, he's on our side. I love you, man. I really do. In fact I feel love coming from everybody in this room. No, I really do. Everyone, and we love you back. I love you back. This is wonderful. Truly wonderful. What can I say? I'm honored, that's what I can say. Truly honored. Honored. Such love in this room, and we're going to go the distance and win."

With that everyone stood—they'd been provided chairs this day—and screamed their lungs dry. People from the streets poured into the place filling the aisles and pumping their signs up and down.

"Take back our country!"

"Take back our country!"

"Take back our country!"

"Now," Dyl continued, "I wonder what these noodle heads will print tomorrow when they hear what I'm going to say today? Everyone else in this race is using PACs and SuperPACs for support. Don't let them kid you. These guys will be beholden to those supporters when it comes to what they decide to do on the major and minor issues both. They are, in effect, figureheads. People on strings. I'm not. I'm funding my own campaign. I have no one to answer to except you, the people. So I say, 'Take back our country!'"

The crowd leapt to their feet and chanted again. "Take back our country!" and pumped their signs, and blew their candidate kisses. Dyl had entered the big time now, and loved it. Simply loved it. So simple. So very, very simple. Nothing works better than giving people what they want. To Take back *their* country!

"So," he continued, "we're going to build that wall and let the world fight fights between themselves as we spend our money where it belongs, right here, making things right again. This election's going to be a game changer. We're going to build our armies so strong, so strong, so very strong, that no one's going to come near us.

"We're going to take care of those bridges so they won't collapse, and those roads that won't sink during the next rainstorm, and build our armies to defeat anyone. We're going to once again reap the rewards that come from democracy of the people, by the people, and for the people. And who are those people?"

"We are."

"You bet we are. Because we're going to 'take back our country!"

"Take back our country!"

"Take back our country!"

"Because I'm not taking a penny, not a penny, from anyone. I listen to you, the people, not some billionaire that inherited his money and power from his daddy, but someone who built his fortune honestly and from scratch. No one controls Dylan Frye except you, the people."

"Take back our country!"

"You alone do I listen to."

"Take back our country!"

"Take back our country!"

"We're going to make the nation right again, like the founders intended it to be. Not weak and incompetent as those now in charge, but strong. The greatest country in the history of the world."

"Take back our country!"

"Take back our country!"

"We love you. I can feel the love in this room. I really can. People say I'm not a nice person. Not a nice person. But *you* know, you really do. I *am* a nice person. Really. I am. Together we're going to 'Take back our country!'"

The room shook for a second time with applause, screaming, foot stomping, and sign waving. So what if the average IQ was low. Those with brains had had their chance and look where it's brought us. Back to the dark ages. War around the world. Terrorism. Could as well have been the Third World War because the world was certainly involved. So he told them that.

"Listen, folks, everyday we pick up our newspapers and watch our TVs about how something or other, a bomb maybe, has gone off somewhere in the world. Never know where it's going to happen next. Unlike the first two world wars, the third is crawling up behind us and not one of those Washington notices. We're pandering to the world of insane people. No more, I tell you. No more. No more. Let them destroy what's theirs if they want. Not us. No Third World War here. We're Taking back our country!'"

"Take back our country!"

"Take back our country!"

"Believe me we will. Like we should. Regain the power that's rightfully ours and once again we'll be looked up to as the best of the best. The war will stop because everyone will see what democracy run intelligently can do."

"Take back our country!"

The next day's headlines read, "Frye Declares Third World War." "Frye Admits He's Beholden to Himself." "Frye Says We're In The Dark Ages." All great headlines because the first word in each was his last name. Everything he said became a twelve-point or pica size, usually near the top of the front page under the name of the paper. First story for the talking heads.

He'd definitely begun the ride in earnest. To the finish line for sure.

27. Competitors

The polls started coming out immediately, showing a mess of a race between Frye and his seven competitors. Surprisingly, Dyl didn't appear first, but fourth out of eight. But Tom smiled instead of frowning. "You're in the polls and you're not last. Great news. Right in the middle of the pack, Dyl. Perfect. You've got your goals set out for you and away we go. You'll be first before you know it."

As always, Tom was right as rain.

Requests for personal interviews came in truckloads, and Dyl, per Tom's instructions, agreed to every one of them granted that he would make his answers short and differentiate between interviewer and guests who had questions. In the first case, answer directly and to the point. In the second case, respond with as much vagueness as possible.

As per the first, an example would be, "You've said that you're funding your campaign on your own dime. Is that correct?"

"Yes."

"How much is it costing?"

"Nothing so far."

"How can that be?"

"So many people want interviews. So many people. What can I say? You're paying, not me."

As per the second, an example would be, "You told one caller that you felt that being a prisoner of war didn't necessarily make one a hero. Well my father suffered as a prisoner of war in support of his country. Is he not a hero?"

"Repeat that last part, will you?"

"Is he not a hero?"

"Well, as I see it, you're absolutely right. Absolutely right. Next question?"

To those pundits who asked him about his schedule being too filled with interviews and speeches, Dyl responded that, "I love it, I really do. Wonderful people with wonderful questions. It's great. No, I really mean it. It doesn't cost me a thing. Really. My campaign has cost me nothing. Everything without PACs or SuperPACs. Let me tell you, this is truly fun. It is. It really is fun. No reason to spend money if I don't have to. This is how I'll take back our country!"

Back home, Katrina lived with her servants and her children visited once in a while. She had been born a trophy kid, a trophy teenager, both in Vienna no less, and didn't mind being the occasional trophy wife to Dyl, the next President of the United States. All she had to do was smile, dress up in skintight weekly new wardrobes, and fake orgasms once or twice a month to live the life of a princess. The old world had never been as good as this.

Every so often Dyl would take her along on one of his trips across country and she did nothing but smile and buy more dresses, shoes, hats, and various undergarments that pleased her husband no end. So what that he'd make a comment occasionally about how good he had it in bed with her, that he'd make it with their grown up daughter if she wasn't his own child, and compare her boobs with those of the other candidate's wives. Everything in fun and whatever he did was fine with her. She made good money from it. Who cared?

The press loved Dyl even if he expressed only vile hatred for them. He thought it strange. It didn't make sense that this would occur. Like water running uphill. The more he told his raving lunatic audiences how much he detested the cameramen who were only doing what they were told, the more they showed up to his events.

The hecklers, though, the ones sent he was sure by the opposing candidates of his own party no less, now they were something else.

"Throw the bums out. Hate me, do they, well what are they doing here then? Throw 'em out, I tell you. Out. Out." Follow that with, "Makes it fun though, doesn't it? We always have a good time here. A really good time. Dylan can throw a good party, can't he? Come to a Frye's party and you're going to have a good time. Throw the bum out. Get him out of here. That's right."

Scuttlebutt had it in the press that Dylan had hired the hecklers himself. With his own money. The same money he hadn't spent on his campaign. Supposedly that is.

Debates did not prove as effective a vehicle for Dylan as he thought they might. He and Tom had to work late at night to figure out ways to answer questions that he had no idea how to answer. Most of these questions involved world issues that required knowledge of kings, emperors, and princes that ran countries he'd never heard of. Who knew, for example, that llham Aliyev was the President of Azerbaijan or that Charles Savarin held the same office for Dominica. For God's sake, there were almost two hundred recognized countries, and every day it seemed another one would fall or another added.

So, rather than memorizing the countries and their leaders and their views and their religions and their relationships with their neighbors, Dyl and Tom spent their time on answers that sounded right but so vague as to provide no information whatsoever. Examples included, "I can't really say, since I haven't seen him in sometime and he might have changed his views since then," and, "He's not clear on where he stands and that may be part of the problem," and, "I got some news today but because of my schedule I haven't yet had time to read it. Will have to wait," and, "I don't think that's a proper question to ask someone in my position," and, "I've read your newspaper's views on these things you bring up and for the most part agree with them," and "Do you know where the men's room is?" with this last one used only if everything else failed.

The two of them, Dyl and Tom, also spent time pouring over photos of Dyl in different poses expressing deep thought, concern, happiness, outrage, frustration, joy, appreciation, and a multitude of other emotions and decided to change some, keep some, and embellish others. The idea here was to ensure that no one spoke with Dylan Frye and felt that his mind had taken a vacation. Everyone knew when they'd asked a question or expressed themselves in some way that he had taken what they said applying the greatest attention possible. In fact, they'd worked out several automatic replies if someone caught him in a mental vacation. For example, "Well that's a good one, I've never heard of it before," or, "Maybe I've misunderstood, could you state yourself one more time?" or, "I believe you, I really do," or, "Where are you going with this?" or, "So who do you think is responsible?"

In short, by the time the two of them finished, Dyl had a collection of sentences to memorize that would not only get him out of any predicament he might find himself in, but that he could be saying something of meaning without actually saying anything. There was an art to it. Dyl would master it as any good politician would and should.

28. Dropouts

The first full month of the race had one candidate drop out, another take a leave of absence whatever that meant, and Dylan now second of the six real candidates left in his party for the Presidency of the U.S.

Of course, Dyl had stepped in it a few times, but hey, who hasn't. The problem with Dylan's stepping in things he shouldn't be stepping in was that when he stepped in them they splashed bigger and longer than when anyone else did. For him that meant that the other candidates were wimps. At the same time, however, he did belong to a party for what that was worth, and that party was now resolving to toss him out on his butt. He'd always been an outlier, but running a third party candidacy this far into the game would prove suicidal for his path to success. At the same time, though, he was not going to go to anyone on bended knee.

"We've got to get back on the same page with them, Tom," Dylan said when they'd found a place to be alone together.

"Why?"

"They're talking about throwing me out."

"Perfect."

"Why?"

"Because they can't."

"Why not?"

"They'd be biting off their own head to save their hide. Committing suicide. Your fans would follow you and halve the party which would lose not only the top office in the land but most likely the Senate and the house as well. We'd be a three party system with two of those parties half of their previous ones."

"So they're bluffing."

"You bet they are."

"So what do we do?"

"Call their bluff. Prove that you're bigger and better than they are. You have the money. You have the love of your fans. You have the power though you may not know it."

"I have those things?"

"You do."

"Wow. So how do I call their bluff?"

"Ignore them like they don't exist. Give whoever asks about them one of your, our, vacuous answers. Or state unequivocally that the country should let them do what they will. You'll win either way. Say it convincingly enough that they'll believe you. Think you can do that?"

"You bet I can."

"Go to it."

Dyl did, and they believed him. They *really* believed him. Dyl learned quickly the power of saying you have the power. The Washington establishment was a bunch of pussies. He could blow their house down in a matter of seconds. At least that's what they believed, and that's the only thing that mattered.

The first debate, with six active candidates, hit the scales with fifteen million viewers, so incendiary had Dyl made his open attacks on his competitors. He thought the estimate was low and therefore promised himself to raise the temperature a few degrees to bring attention to those that had opted for other more traditional programs.

The first question to Dyl sounded like he'd created it himself.

"So, Mister Frye, What do you think is the most important issue that you would address were you to get the nomination?"

"A weakened military is what I think. The current and outgoing administration had no idea what they're doing. Like their still attempting to talk peace with the Japanese after Pearl Harbor. Give me a break. We need to beef up our military to make sure we have a country in the first place. Without the country, there's nothing else to do. Number one? Produce the greatest and most powerful country in the world. The biggest and best and we'll do that by . . ."

"Times up."

"Screw that. We need to double our military's size and give them the best weapons possible so that they . . ."

"Times up, Mister Frye."

"So that they can double down on any other five countries that might want to . . ."

"Times up, I said, Mister Frye."

" . . . attack us. If we don't have a country, no other issue matters. You see that . . ."

"Mister Welsh, do you have a comment?"

"Our economy is a dead issue if we don't exist. We must be strong . . . "

" . . . in order to . . . "

"Mister Frye. You have to adhere to the rules. We've heard your response."

" . . . continue to be a player on the stage . . ."

"Cut his microphone someone, will you?"

On it went, with Dylan towering as the alpha male of the group not taking anything from anyone for anything.

"Mister Frye, could you summarize your positions in twenty words or less?"

" . . . we need to take care of our vets. *Really* take care of them. What we're doing now is hopeless. Hopeless you hear? How do you expect our fighting men to go to the battlefields and fight for their country when they know that their wounds against an enemy determined to kill them gets better treatment after the war they will. We have to pour as much resources as we can into the military and our vets. Show them what we're made of. Not like these wussies on stage with no propose. No better than the current administration, I tell you. No, I really mean it. They'll talk you to death before shooting the first bullet. Everything is appeasement. That's not the way to get things accomplished. I tell you . . . "

"Mister Welsh, do you have some closing words for us?"

" . . .that military might . . ."

"Cut his microphone, Ralph."

The news the next day ping-ponged back and forth like never before. Some for and some against the riotous debate that Dyl had attempted to kidnap before America's eyes. By the time the next one came around, the audience had doubled in preparation for one hell of a wrestling match between Dylan Frye and the rest of the candidates who had no idea how to counter the man who wouldn't quit talking.

By this time, Dylan had vaulted himself into first place, and not by a couple of percentage points but into a double figure lead over the rest of the pack. He'd broken the rules and gotten points for it rather than demerits.

Tom, of course, was pleased with the results in terms of the rankings, but disgusted with Dyl for his non-stop self-indulgence. A speech, talk as long as your voice held out. Questions in an interview, which these debates qualified as, short answers like, "Increase our military spending. Without a strong military we're going down." Simple as that. Somehow, the cameras and the knowledge that he was reaching millions alongside the competition, had given Dyl the idea that he had to keep the attention centered on him and let the others be damned.

They spoke about it, argued, and Dyl agreed to tone it down the next time.

Good luck with that.

29. Knives

The second debate's questioning began with the least ranked candidate in the bunch. He did what most politicians did under these circumstances following the Gospel according to Dyl, he wishy-washed himself through both sides of the issue so that no one could convict him of anything but being indecisive.

It quickly became obvious to Dyl that he would be the last one. No problem, he thought, save the best for last. Him. Gave him more of a chance to play off the other answers, comment on them, and drive in the knife blade to the heart.

The first question had been, "What would you do to restart the economy?" By the time that question reached him, Dylan was damned ready to answer it. But first, of course, he had a few gems up his sleeve.

"My esteemed colleagues, though I should leave 'esteemed' out of my description because they are cowards to a one, haven't answered the question. Why? Because, as I say, they're cowards. They don't want to be President, they want to crawl around on their hands and knees begging for your votes by first taking this point of view and then that point of view. Full of crap, I say. The economy? Easy. Bring back the jobs the companies are taking away from us by building their factories in foreign countries to get cheap labor. Hell, I'd do it were I not a true American first and foremost. And how do we do that? Easy. Raise the taxes on the imports of those companies by two hundred percent, that's how. They'll come back with their tails between their legs and never think about doing such things again. Our jobless rates go down and our economy goes up to the top. Hell, beyond the top. What's with these idiots that they can't see this? The people out there without jobs see it. I see it. Hell, probably they see it now that I've said it. They, meaning them!" Dylan pointed at his competition and jeered at them. "These numbskulls can't add two and two to get four. Why anyone would vote for any one of them over me is beyond my comprehension. You gotta understand, I've been doing this kind of business most my life. I know how it works. I'm the greatest businessman the world has ever known. You want economy, I got economy. It's so simple. Vote for me."

Dyl had gone overtime by several minutes with his rant, but the questioner being paid to ask questions and keep the time straight was too mesmerized to keep score.

When the debate had finished, every pundit in sight had declared Dyl the winner. His lead grew overnight, and the number of interview requests and speech invitations doubled. He accepted every one of them. Why not? Dylan loved to talk. About anything. Even to those who hated him as well as those who loved him. He was reaching for the stars, he thought, and no piss ants here on earth could stop he who would be king from getting what he truly wanted.

Power.

"Notice I don't read off teleprompters or notes. I don't need to have someone else write what I'm going to say. I say it. Like I don't need someone else to pay my bills. What you see and hear is what you get. My competitors don't know or remember what they believe or stand for. They need to be reminded, right down to the last word. Give me a break. What kind of President do you want, my friends? Someone controlled by people you've never heard of behind the scenes, or by the person you voted for because you believe he's right?"

This off-the-cuff-and-without-teleprompters speech addition that Dyl had included for the hell of it rang so true that some of the other candidates fell for his bull. He knew it was bull. Not that he didn't have good ideas, but because he had no idea of the complexities of the government and how they could be carried out. He made things sound as if all he had to do was to say them and his slaves in the various committees would carry them out without question. He didn't know how the government worked. His fans loved that about him. He loved himself for being the way he was. Truth be known, he'd fail the first day in office and most likely fail every day until he was either impeached, murdered by his staff, or carted off to the asylum.

There was a part of Dyl, a small part yes but a part nonetheless, that understood this. But he had a way of putting things off that bothered him. Placing them neatly in a mental stack in the back of his mind that he would get to when the getting became possible. Trouble was, the getting was never possible.

The day would come that it might be necessary, and that day, the day he became President of the U.S. of A, the hens would come home to roost and Dylan Frye would have to confront the fact that as President there were limits to what he could achieve by his lonesome.

But that day would be long in coming. Plenty of time. Now was the time to have fun. To give his fans the ride of their lives. To so work his way to a landslide victory that it would make history. The non-politician that would take the political office that ran the world.

Of course his competition wasn't that keen on him making it the full distance, so they argued at first to no avail, and so attempted to shoot from the hip, unaware apparently of Dyl's motto to 'get even,' and get even he got. Without much of a lapse of time between insult and injury, the former his and the latter theirs as an integral part of his strategy brought about not by the electrical conduits of his brain, but his less logical chemical ones, the ones that doctors sell plenty of to keep the pharmaceutical companies rolling in dough.

"Maybe Mister Frye's inexperience and thus incompetence in these matters is showing," one of his debating partners suggested as a part of his answer to another question.

"You know, Mister Chairman, I'm worried about the Senator. His left eye is twitching mercilessly and I maybe be out of line here but thinking about his long term health, it might be good to query the audience to see if we have any doctors present in the house."

Things like that led to others of a more grievance provoking nature.

"Mister Chairman, I believe that Mister Frye is attempting to lower the IQ of this debate with his remarks."

"May I suggest, Mister Chairman, that the Senator has already done that by showing up tonight."

And worse.

"How can Mister Frye say such things about my wife?"

"Because I've seen her undressed, Senator, and never want to repeat that experiment again let me tell you."

The ratings for the debates grew to record heights. No matter how low things got, Dyl somehow had the ability to pull them lower. While many of his competitors attempted to remember their memorized lines taught them by their begging staffs, they forgot them and tried to best a man who could fling the horseshit better and faster than they could.

American politics had long forgotten the early days when such things were common, so even the most erudite of those still watching were shocked by the back alley antics that Frye seemed expert at driving the conversation down and into.

"Your son's showing signs of playing around with other male children's dinguses in the little boys room."

"If your wife's boobs dropped any lower she could use them to sweep the floors."

"How often do you get your toenails manicured, Senator?"

"Who's that I saw you with last night, she looked like a retard. I hope it wasn't your wife."

"I see you survived your autopsy, Senator,' and they found whatever they were looking for."

On and on and on. Dylan had no idea where he got these things, but 'getting even' was getting even and as he watched, his competitors grew more and more wary of continued dueling with the king of crap. The public, however, was insatiable. Never too much for them.

Some of his comments, though, even proved too much, especially for the diehards. Like, "Women belong in the kitchen, why else would they have been born knowing how to cook?' showing his misogynist side, or "No daughter of mine's going to marry a black, their dicks are too God damned big," showing his racist side. Or, "Make' em wear armbands, I tell you, worked for the Germans during the Second World War," showing his anti-Semitic self. Everyone knew that these epithets were off the charts when it came to proper decent behavior, but those following him forgave him or thought he was joking, or agreed with him enough to make them cling closer to their hero who had the audacity to break the most powerful PC rules ever established.

All these aphorisms, of course, added up to someone full of angst and hatred that should have brought one Dylan Frye to his knees. The only thing they'd done, though, was to bring the already angry populace to fever pitch. As mean as rattlers on steroids. Crowds for his speeches reached heights larger than any before him running for the highest office. Even when he'd tell his staff on the same day that he'd decided to give one that afternoon and they scurried about like mice in heat, he drew thousands upon thousands eager, if nothing else, for at least a change from the normal boring examples they'd put up with for so long.

Many in the group had drifted over from the other party. They'd tired of the same ol', same ol', and wanted at least some laughs. But that, of course, led to disagreements among members of the audience to which Dyl encouraged those involved to beat the shit out of one another. This brought the cops and once again, Dyl had outdone himself. Elmer Gantry should have it so good. Dylan would often be hours late, arriving with his entourage long after the scheduled start time. Everyone stuck around. In fact it gave those who might be late to come, and those who happened to be in the neighborhood, time to stop and to see what the hullaballoo was all about. A perfect example of antisocial behavior producing larger audiences and more potential voters for the alpha male of his party.

The Internet grew during this time in the sense that data about the man of the hour, the most loved and hated man in the history of the world, went off the chart. He was compared to Hitler, Goldwater, Wallace, McCarthy, Mussolini, Napoleon, Caesar, Stalin, Pol Pot, Idi Amin, Caligula, Nero, Genghis Khan, Franco, and many that Dyl had never hear of, no less had any idea what they'd done.

30. The Hate Factor

The relationship between Dyl and his competitors steadily worsened, if that was possible. Dylan had no compunctions about arguing personal problems that had little to do with campaigns, issues, or competency. In every case, though, Dyl didn't rise to the occasion, his competitors lowered themselves further into the muck that Dyl's mind had slowly dove into. With this, the riff between Tom and Dyl grew wider, slowly but steadily.

"You're winning the nomination, Dyl, but what you don't understand is that by doing it the way you're doing it, you're going to lose the general. Hell, I think half your wins are due to those from the other party crossing over to vote for you."

"So what? That's a good thing, isn't it?"

"No. It isn't. They're doing it because they want you to win the nomination because they know if you do, their voters will get out the vote and handily beat you. So, your short-run plan is only as good as it helps your long-range plan."

"But if I lose in the short run, Tom, I automatically lose in the long run. Don't you see?"

"I do. But there are many ways to win, Dyl, and most of those don't involve any of the things you're doing. See my point?"

"No, I don't."

"Most attacks that politicians make are, say, above the line."

"What line?"

"The line that separates decency from indecency. The line between getting dirty and class."

"So you're saying I don't have class?"

"No. I'm saying that you're acting like you don't have class. There's a difference."

"Ah, political correctness. PC. I hate that. We should be allowed to say what we think. Exactly what we think. Not sugar coat it with pleasantries."

"I get that, Dyl, I really do. But when it goes south, there's no sugar left. You're right down in the sewer with the diseased rats and other vermin. I know you don't want that."

"You telling me I'm swimming with the sharks? If you are, that's exactly where I want to be, Tom. I want people to believe that I'm strong, resilient, and ready to take the battle to the enemy."

"Fine. But it's a good idea along the way to make sure you know who your friends are as well. Don't lump them in with your enemies."

"I'm not."

"You are when you shoot from the hip and wound or knock off anyone near you in the process. Get the point?"

"No."

They argued for hours after that.

Meanwhile, the field reduced itself to three candidates, the others out of funding, having lost their SuperPACs or worn down to the nub from the constant supply of attacks leveled at them by the frontrunner. Dyl's own party had grown tired of the mire in which he'd drawn everyone around him into. They planned a number of retributions including, of course, attempting to undermine the party's convention to somehow ensure that he didn't get the required votes for a nomination on the first ballot, leaving almost anything free to occur if that happened.

Meanwhile again, Dyl had his backup team working hard promising the candidates that had backed out of continuing their run for the presidency that he would appoint them to various posts including VP if they would publically back his run and suggest that the delegates they'd won vote for him instead of others still in the race. These people, once on board, followed Dylan around and introduced him at his public speaking events not realizing that by doing so they were acquiescing to what appeared to audiences something he'd demanded them to do. Thus, more vivid proof of Dyl's strength and power.

Amidst this chaos, the debates, building his delegate count, attacks from the competition and his own party as well as the one he opposed, his now ongoing fight with Tom, getting even, getting charged by groups of the various 'isms' they'd decided he represented, the press, litigation from those who felt wronged at his rallies by being attacked by his supporters, his various entrepreneurial enterprises going down the toilet, his fortune being ravaged though he would never admit it, and numerous other things going right or wrong didn't matter which, Dyl invited himself to see another psychiatrist on the sly so as to help him get some sleep without nightmares and to rid him of this nagging desire to run wildly into the forest somewhere, drooling and puking his way to madness. Something was wrong. He'd always loved chaos before, making it happen when it was lacking to help him feel real.

This time he found a new one. Not someone who only gave him pills. Not someone who he'd have another affair with or, God forbid divorce his wife for and marrying a fourth time. A transvestite or something that probably knew more about the state of his mind than anyone else did. Who knew?

"So, describe one of these nightmares."

"I can describe them. I'm running. I'm always running."

"Away from or toward something?"

"Both."

"Describe first the away part."

"Okay. A mob."

"What kind of mob?"

"There are different kinds of mobs?"

"Sure. There's the mob of evil origins that run brothels, drugs, and so on. There's a mob that gathers around after a murder and wants to hang the man they think is the murderer."

"The second kind."

"The manic kind?"

"Huh?"

"The one that's not professional but gathers on its own on the spur of the moment."

"That's it."

"Tell me about it."

"Right. Well, there's not much to say. But no matter how fast I run they're there behind me."

"That's how your dream begins?"

"Dreams. Yes."

"So you don't know why they're mad at you?"

"Nope."

"Have any ideas?"

"No. That's why I'm here."

"Okay. Then what?"

"They start chasing me."

"And you run?"

"Yes."

"Do they catch you?"

"They're about to, but I wake up."

"That's it?"

"Yes. That's it."

"All of your dreams consist of that?"

"Mostly."

"Okay, what do the ones that don't fall into the mostly part involve?"

"They never get close enough to catch me."

"I see."

"What?"

"What do I see?"

"Yes."

"I see that this is a very common dream that people have. Everyone has at one time or another."

"But mine line up like ducks in a carnival shooting gallery. One after another. One I could take. Hundreds of them, night after night, Doc, they're driving me crazy, I tell you."

"Okay. Now I get it. It's not so much the dream itself, but the fact that you have it every night."

"Yes. Driving me crazy. What's wrong with me?"

"My guess?"

"Yes."

"You're cracking up."

"That the official name for it?"

"Not exactly. I called it that because it means you're in too deep and your brain is trying to tell you that. You need to take a vacation. Something that'll put you in contact with nature again. A nice relaxing vacation."

"How can I do that? I'm running for President."

"I understand that. But you'll never make it there unless you take a break. A week would help. You can afford taking a week can't you?"

"I don't know. A week's a long time when you're running for President."

"I suppose it is. Of course I could give you some pills to relax you. They might help."

"Instead of a vacation?"

"Well it would be better with 'and a vacation,' but they will help without a vacation, too."

"What kind of pills?"

"Not drugs. Pills that will up your dopamine, the natural drug that your body may not be providing enough of to cope with your schedule at this point."

"What if they don't work?"

"They will."

"How can you be sure?"

"Because, as I say, they work using your own system rather than by making you sleepy or things like that."

"Perfect, Doc, so my dreams will go away?"

"I never make promises about dreams. They have a life of their own. What I'm given you in those pills, though, will make your life easier and thus I can't imagine them not helping you sleeping better as a result."

"Thanks, Doctor."

31. Pills

It took roughly four hours before the press got hold not only of Dyl's visit to a psychiatrist, but the exact prescription that he'd recommended, the latter by enlarging frames from cameras within the drug store where he'd gone to have it filled. His first visit to a different psychiatrist had not received such attention since Dyl had not at that time been the major figure he'd become at this point.

Headlines read as, "Frye Using Prescription Drugs to Relax," and ""Frye seeks Psychiatric Help," and, well, you can pretty much imagine the rest.

This creepy feeling that Dyl had no private life any longer didn't help his sleeping much and forced him to take double doses of both his original sleeping pills and his new prescription on the sly by using the basement with the lights off, assuming that his life had been invaded by every form of electronic contraption known to man by this point.

If one were to have to choose from the many assaults that ignited action from Dylan's arsenal of verbal munitions, 'getting even' would be the one. So, without the slightest hesitation, Dyl fired back with not one but two bursts of his cannons in the direction of the press, the evil press, out for nothing except 'outing' one or more of the candidates, didn't matter which to them.

Using one of his favorite supermarket tabloids as the vehicle, he charged the most guilty newspaper with both slanderous lies and informing them that their reporter, the one most responsible for the story, of having sex with monkeys in his spare time. So outrageous was this accusation, that the very paper who employed the reporter that ran the story as a headline, rebuked Dyl's charge. Of course it didn't matter that the denials flew left and right, Dyl had already won the war. His name had once again topped the headlines and, once again, the newspaper who'd leaked the original story by siding with their own reporter, had given it legs.

But Dyl was far from through. Who knew when such a thing might surface again? He had to turn off this spigot at the source for the duration. So he pulled out all the stops by leaking another story with the rest of the press that the head of the newspaper that published the original story on Dyl regularly mutilated his wife and children by sticking pencils and other things like carrots, string beans, and bananas, up their vaginas or anuses without provocation to do so. Didn't matter whether it wasn't true. Didn't matter he'd get sued. What mattered was that the story about Dyl got lost in the chaos and the various people involved realized quickly that they'd run up against a pro and they were amateurs.

All this action somehow made Dyl rest easier, sleep better, and his nightmares went away. He didn't need the dope. Getting even *was* his dope. A few days rest, realizing he might lose the election, and so on, had driven him to it. Now he was back on his own turf again. The election didn't really matter. What mattered was that he'd proved he was the biggest bully on the block and could throw the shit better than anyone in the world. If that wasn't a high qualification for being President, what was?

Of course, Tom was livid. For him it was like watching sumo wrestlers slipping and sliding in Jell-O as ladies of the night might do but far less excitingly so. Flabs of fat wobbled and earthquakes shook the room as the fighters attempted to get in next shots. Dyl may be having his jollies, but Tom was slowly igniting his campaign with Poe-like images of raven-owls crowing 'who, who?'

Thus, the first significant fallout from the most recent mud thrown was Tom's resignation from Dyl's campaign staff. The farewell went short and sweet, with both shaking hands tentatively, saying nothing, and Tom taking the box of things that were his to the door and out, thankful to be leaving something that had gone well beyond the borders of decency in his view. Dyl liked the thought of watching his long held partner vanish from view, knowing that his berating criticisms would allow him, Dyl, to join the ranks as one of the greatest rat fuckers in the history of American politics.

While this was transpiring, the field of candidates reduced to two with Dyl still heavily in the lead but his competition not mathematically eliminated from the race completely. Still a chance of something unexpected giving the idiot a mathematical possibility to overtake Dyl at the last minute.

So on top of his spat with the press, Dyl had the joy of tossing a grenade into the life of his one remaining threat before nomination at the convention. His name was Norman Calhoun, a southern Baptist of some wealth that had still hung onto his money and used a primarily evangelical base to build his constituency.

Dyl hated Calhoun, not only because of his southern roots and ridiculous Biblical quotations, but mostly because the man looked like a furry white edition of a sheep being readied for the slaughter. No strength, no manhood, no guts. Like some kind of fairy dancing through Mendelssohn's Midsummer Night's Dream. Dyl hated dreams, therefore making it a slam-dunk.

The first salvo at Calhoun involved his mother who, word had it, had screwed a black man that led to his birth. Dyl didn't announce this himself, though, too incendiary, so he used the rumor mill and an anonymous source for a viral-bound video that showed the act being carried out in high-priced animation for everyone to see.

Calhoun, having escaped such shots in the past by being one of the other candidates and attempting to rise about the fray, went ballistic and developing a stammer, quickly falling off the candidate train after a week of attempting to explain to his wife how he'd most likely used some kind of lotion each day to look like a white man instead of what he was. A closet mulatto.

To this, Dyl's fans cheered, his enemies jeered, and most of American feared the distant possibility that Dyl would somehow find a way into the President's office and make the country the laughing stock of the world, inviting the weakest of terrorist-bound countries to take advantage of his weakest points. Every one of them. No experience, no knowledge, no smarts, no staff, no nothing. So his party, and pretty much everyone else including the other party, decided this couldn't be happening and several plans developed that involved everything from assassination, to abandoning the convention entirely and creating a new party from scratch with their own candidate, to working out the impeachment processes ahead of time so that they could begin on Dyl's first day in office.

Meanwhile, the race to pick up a majority of the delegates raged on.

"How did Calhoun pick up thirteen delegates in Colorado last night?" Frye asked Tom's replacement, a guy also named Tom but without *cajones*.

"The good old fashioned way. Bought them."

"What do you mean by that?"

"Bought them? I guess I mean he bought them."

"This is America. I mean it, Tom. How's that legal?"

"He didn't do it by giving them money outright, he had some staff joker take them out to dinner, or buy them into the convention, or promised them something they wanted like a free flight to and from the convention. Lots of ways. No harm in showing them a good time while preaching the Gospel according to Winslow to them."

"Why aren't *we* doing that? Why didn't you tell me we could do that?"

"I did."

"When?"

"During the Ohio run."

"What'd I say?"

"You told me you couldn't be bothered with the little crap, that we only needed the big states to come through. To keep our sights on big numbers, not small ones."

"Why didn't you tell me that the small ones add up?"

"I did. Same night."

"What did I say? Oh forget it. I know what I said. Well I changed my mind, we've got to get the small ones now. It's too close to let the son of a bitch clean up the smaller states."

"Too late."

"What do you mean, too late?"

"They're bought and paid for already."

"So what? We can pay more."

"They're bought and paid for already."

"And I say 'so what?' We'll simply double their price and take them away from the bugger."

"They're already declared, Dyl. Taken. They've signed on to the Winslow bandwagon."

"There must be a way."

"Only if you make them change their declaration. That might work for a couple of them, but not for the whole bunch."

"Let's chop off as many as we can get away with no matter how much it costs. Two more for us is also two less for him. That's four if my arithmetic is right. We punch a hole in enough of these, and we'll win this out."

"It might cost you a bundle."

"How much?"

"Depends on how many we can wrestle away from the guy. If we were to get ten, say, it might be a million or so."

"For ten votes?"

"Twenty according to your math."

Dylan considered it. "Okay. But try to keep it as much under that as you can. Resources are getting tighter and tighter."

"Right."

The ugly delegate wrestling continued as the words by both candidates matched the ferocity and word choice. Dylan took to naming his rival 'Big Blow' Winslow. 'Big Blow' Winslow this. 'Big Blow' Winslow that.

32. Sticking

First on the agenda, however, was to make sure that Dyl lost the election. Thus, both parties decided on a bit of crossing the aisle, or bipartisanship. A strange time for this to occur given the many important bills that stalled in Congress or never got signed by the President, but a necessary evil that both detested but both required. When it came to survival, both wanted that equally.

The major problem, of course, was that you could sling the mud at Dylan, but none of it stuck. It slide down his slippery self to the ground faster than it had ridden through the air on its way to him. The guy was immune to attacks. Worse yet, he thrived on it. Everything anyone could dig up on the man made his followers that much more determined to help him win the election. Even those who hated the man found him so funny that they would watch his speeches and debates more than their own candidate's speeches and debates. Everything they tried worked against them rather than for them. Dyl obviously had some kind of magic that, like Superman, accelerated him rather than slowing him down. They needed at least a pound of Kryptonite in the worst way.

With the nomination in his pocket, Dyl only needed to wait until the convention and pull out all the stops on his opponent, whoever that might be since three were still vying for the opposing party's nomination with none having the necessary votes for the victory. An open convention looked assured and Dyl loved the fact that he'd have extra time on his hands to plot his final push when the time came.

Of course, with his sleep deprivation under control and his obvious need for taking shots at someone, he grew restless quickly and longed for someone other than his own party's idiots who were arguing over how to tear his campaign apart.

So, as one might imagine, he decided to take part in some target practice. Warm up by tearing apart the two opposing party's candidates he didn't want to win the nomination so that the one he knew he could beat in the general would survive. It was a typical Dylan Frye trick and you'd have thought the powers that be should recognize but didn't.

He heaved his first salvo over one of the candidates' backyard fence by buying three doctors who'd claim that the man had a bad ticker, that his heart condition made him unfit for office. None of these doctors had ever seen the man no less examined him, but money talks and the investment proved invaluable. By the time anyone got wise to his little trick, the story would have done its damage and the public forgotten the candidate entirely. No votes, no challenge.

The other guy proved a more difficult nut to crack. Like eating a rare steak without teeth. The trick was to get him, as he had the previous one, to believe that these grenades were coming from the candidate of the other party that had the current lead by a slim margin. A virtual tie. But that evil doing had worked once and might not work twice. So Dyl tossed his next IED at the frontrunner so he could *really* be the culprit in attempting to get even.

It worked, and before long, the other party was as disheveled as his own had been before. Three candidates getting down and dirty and fighting one another like cats in an alley, no holds barred. Garbage for garbage, slime for slime, and pitch for pitch. Dyl felt like the producer he was. Above the fray now, and everyday acting more like the father figure he knew the American public wanted. Power, money, and love, the latter he'd forgotten but now turned on the juice.

"I love my fans," he told a reporter for the Times. "They're the very best, I tell you. The very, very best. Loyal? I tell you the most loyal fans in the world. They'd vote for me if I shot one of them dead for the hell of it. Prove my guts and power. We like that. We really, really do. Well, the most important thing that anyone would do in the kind of a position we're talking about here, is to find out what's on the minds of those most effected by whatever you do. Get their opinions. Make a list."

On and on and on.

He kept his name in the press, often more than his opponent to be, whose opposition had vanished by now. Life was good at the top, but boring and getting more so by the moment. His medication had done the job and he was ready to get into it with someone, anyone. The only one still standing that meant anything would have to be the victim. Ahead of schedule.

Dyl nibbled around the edges. A few practice shots to see how the presumptive nominee of the other party would react. Like an unnamable source claiming the man had had an affair. Simple. Not an affair with a goat, or an alien, or a man, but an affair, and what he thought would bring no reaction or a reactive shot in return given the man could guess who the unnamed source was, he instead got an immediate flurry of claims of innocence and more than suggestive warnings of litigation. 'Methinks thou dost protest too much,' from Hamlet came to mind.

Dylan backed off at that, for it was true that becoming President by acclimation with his opponent not showing up for the bout gave his ego a boost, the public wouldn't go for it. He could hear his old Tom in the distance warning him to lay off. So lay off he did.

But here he was, on the precipice of gaining the highest and most powerful position in the world, with nothing much to do but wait. Waiting, of course, being first on the list of the things Dylan hated. So, more than any other thing, Dyl wondered what in hell he could do instead of going crazy before he had a chance to prove to everyone, even his dead parents, maybe most of all them, that he could dance with the best of them. The devil in hell, if need be.

He got it. Choose his cabinet and his team starting now and then announce a new one every day to the press. It would bring the media down on him, deflate his opponent the more, and generally prove to the public that he was worthy of the post to which they were about to elect him to.

To further help his ultimate campaign and to work it so that his time in office would have the least amount of angst, he did a whistle-stop tour of the country in support of candidates of his party for Congress. This would ensure that bills he proposed and they proposed would go through without a hitch since they'd have a majority of both Senate and house.

33. Slings And Arrows

When Dylan suffered the slings and arrows of his opponents, he smiled as he simultaneously planned devious ways to get even. When the press attempted to make a fool out of him, he laughed and told them they were only making fools of themselves, and the more confident he got in making that work, the more regal he became in his immediate reaction, acting like a man who could not be bothered with such trivial matters. This, of course, made him yet more popular among nearly everyone. Except his own party, the one who did not want he who would be king to be king.

So, as his popularity grew and sang, "Take back our country!"—yes, someone had made a popular song out of his motto—Dyl took on the aurora of a man untouchable in every way. A narcissist of immense proportions that the great Napoleon couldn't counter. America had apparently found its twenty-first century symbol of justice and world domination, and boasted of it being so.

But he was also asked the magic question, the one with the tag 'self-destructing' attached to it in invisible ink. The one to which there was no right answer that would provide anyone with assurance except those few who firmly believed the end of the world was near. And that question, one that had eluded Dyl or that he'd eluded until now was, "Would you use nuclear weapons if the time came to use them?"

Put that way, of course, the answer was easy. "Sure." But the follow up question that came as sure as night the day was the kicker. "When might that time be?" The possible answers to that query exploded in his face every time. So, maybe at the zenith of his popularity and the zenith of his self-confidence, it arrived, neatly packaged in a nice looking reporter who'd obviously taken a turn around this block before and seen the carnage it had produced, for she smiled as she asked it in a way that told Dyl only the Devil himself could have arranged the situation.

The easiest answer, of course, was that one should unleash the nuclear arsenal after the opponent does. But that won't work when the only time you can truly be sure your opponent has done so is after you've been demolished, or at the least, when you know your days are numbered. Anyway you worked the problem, you were either for making the first move, or you weren't, and neither of those two possibilities was acceptable. To anyone. Anywhere. Anytime.

So, of course, Dylan dodged the issue by requesting the reporter ask him again since he missed the middle part somehow. He spent the time she repeated it giving it as much thought as he could and coming up with the same answer everyone else came up with. Nothing.

But Dylan didn't get where he'd gotten by shying away from questions, or so he'd convinced himself.

"I think you're asking that question in the wrong way," he said, attempting to push the problem back onto the lovely reporter who Dyl had noticed had the most beautiful legs of any woman he'd ever seen. Had her publishers sent her to wile her ways on him to confuse him further with her question?

"How would you have me pose it?" she asked him without blinking, and obviously having been prepared by experts.

"I think you're asking me about war," Dyl replied, trying to keep his eyes off those legs.

"No, I'm pretty sure I'm not. I'm asking you about when you'd use nuclear weapons."

"During a war," Dylan said, "all bets are off."

"But what if you're not at war and another country or a random group of terrorists wish to use them, maybe especially when you can't gather the bombs in one place and use them directly but have to kill a lot of innocent people if you retaliate that way?"

'Jesus,' Dyl thought, 'this is getting worse by the second.'

"I'd go for the arsenal and blow the weapons up rather than the people."

Good answer he thought. Let her try and get out of this one.

"What if they'd scattered the weapons they had left around where millions of innocents lived. What would you do?"

Worse yet, he had to bail on this one.

"Listen. You've asked many good questions here, my dear, and I appreciate them. These are the kinds of hard questions that Presidential candidates deserve to be asked. Answering them is like eating unpopped popcorn. Certainly your nuclear threat is a proper test of the merits of any candidate. It really is. Or should I say, they really are. Whatever, you can ask them and I should answer them. It's fair game. As a matter of fact I love these kinds of questions for they are a true test of my abilities to answer them. I never run from questions, my dear, I never do. Ask anyone and you'll get the same answer, I never run from the hard questions. Have you asked that of those who follow me? Have you?"

"No."

"Well you should. You'll find that there's no one out there, for me or against me that believes that I run from questions. I love them. We love them. Questions like these must be asked, I tell you, if we are to ultimately achieve the right kinds of leaders to really do the job. You want that kind of leader don't you miss?"

"I do."

"Well, if you vote for me you'll get one, I can assure you. Now, if you don't mind, and having answered your questions, I have another appointment to tend to. I have many appointments. I'm going to become the President of the United States, young woman. Do you know that?"

"Yes, Sir."

"Good. So the best to you and maybe we'll meet again in the future some time. I hope we do because I love the questions you ask. I really do. Trust me."

Someone then entered the room as Dyl pushed the proper button with his knee and that person showed the young lady out the door and into the lobby where she belonged.

Dyl thought he'd handled that brilliantly.

34. Miscalculations

When Dylan found his interview in the newspaper the next day, he realized the truth of his miscalculation. Everything sounded pretty good for most of the interview except for the final 'nuclear' bomb. There, the reporter had misjudged Dylan and, he supposed, her readers. For she said, "Mister Frye adroitly avoided responding to my question regarding his potential use of nuclear weapons."

He read this three times over and quickly knew he had misjudged her rather than vice versa. Everyone reading this would immediately get the opinion that 'adroitly' meant in this case that Dyl had purposefully avoided answering her question and therefore fearful that answering it truthfully, no doubt sounding more like Goldwater than Carter, wouldn't hesitate to use them whenever he thought necessary, leaving 'necessary' up to her readers to translate.

The headline had been good, the rest of the interview mostly accurate, but that final damn question irritated the hell out of him. Maybe she'd meant it as a compliment, but to him it sounded like an insult through and through.

He called the paper, she was out. Not out of a job but out of the building at the moment. He called her home, she was out. She knew this would bother him and was adroitly avoiding him. Damn bitch. So he wrote a tweet, something he was getting good at, with the hashtag 'adroitly' letting her have it with both barrels. At least letting her have it as much as the number-of-letters limit would let her.

'Don't toy with Dylan,' he wrote, 'you'll get burnt.'

Since he didn't mention the article or the newspaper, most of his followers had no idea what he was talking about. The reporter didn't respond anyway, so he'd shot a blank in her direction.

Maybe.

Dyl, since he'd been compared to the man many times in his recent life, had begun reading about P. T. Barnum, especially the quotes attributed to him. One in particular he loved.

"Clowns are the pegs on which the circus hangs."

Why this particular one caught on with him was confusing. Maybe he thought of himself as a professional clown, loveable and funny. But he looked at others and came up short, though some of the other quotes fit him better. Like, "Without promotion, something terrible happens . . . nothing!" or "Every crowd has a silver lining." Or, "Politics and government are certainly among the most important of practical human interests." But try as he might, the 'Clowns' kept him happy and on track.

He also spent some of his now free time working on his continuing real-estate ventures trying to make more money by putting good after good. He worked the market through his now quite opulent business and when on tour to help get Congress converted to his party. He often stayed in one of his own hotels, taking his lovely wife along as the trophy that she was and liked to be.

However, the thing that continued to bother him most was the rumors that kept flying around about his party. That they were so dedicated to attempting to rid themselves of what they considered, apparently, an unwanted virus, him, that they'd somehow conquered their man.

What had he done to disserve this kind of treatment? After all, he was the one who'd bring the party back into power. Outrageous power. The entire capitol would be his. Or theirs. Or his and theirs.

The riots began innocuously with a kind of bar fight without a bar in one of the aisles of a Dylan Frye stump speech in LA. At first, Dyl thought it might have been deliberately planned by the presumptive nominee of the opposing party, since Dyl hadn't paid anyone to make it happen. But after one punch thrown, the cops hauled the invader out the door and into the streets and everything quieted down except for the cheering Frye fans in the audience.

At the same time and unbeknownst to Dylan, a huge crowd of anti-Frye folks had gathered, chanted, raised signs that read, "Frye Balks But Doesn't Rock," and generally disturbed the peace which, in LA, meant quite a lot. The chanting grew to the point that Dyl could no longer be heard over the din.

While privately he enjoyed the hell out of the mess he was making, he publically and in front of the crowd inside, doubled-down on the obvious visitors, calling them names that many he didn't even know the meaning of. "Turks," "Fascists," "Buggers," "Alchemists," "Assholes," Collaborates," "Idiots," "Immigrants," "Deviates," "Creeps," "Anti-Democratizers," "Racists," and on and on, all of which were broadcast through loudspeakers outside for the crowd of Frye supporters that hadn't shown for fear of reprisals from the group that had shown up and which egged on the riots to the point that they rushed the hall doors and quickly turned what had been a peaceful and derogatory speech by Frye into his quick retreat from the stage and into a chauffer-driven car a city block long and back to his home away from home, one of his hotels. It's giant penthouse to be specific.

All of this because, as Dylan understood it, he'd told a reporter for a recent interview that he would now build a wall around the entire country, including the seashores, so that no one without an explicit permission in writing from him would be allowed through. Maybe worse yet, make everyone non-Aryan wear an arm band identifying themselves for everyone to see and for the cops to take care to vet and interrogate whenever possible, something that both his fans and his staff thought particularly deserved now that the riots had begun. Next step, the army would incur the goose step and make the comparison to the Nazi's a given.

All this, of course, drove Dylan's party to make it a national priority to stop him somehow from becoming the party's nominee to become President of the United States though such a thing seemed highly improbable given Dyl was the only candidate left and the only one having the majority of delegates at the convention.

A special edition of *Mein Kampf* came out, edited by far left socialists in which many comments by Hitler were replaced without much effect on the meaning with similar quotes from Dylan Frye, the presumptive nominee of the party to which he belonged.

It turned out that the convention of Frye's party held a meeting of its Rule's Committee that set the rules for that particular nominating occasion, and that anything and everything was up for grabs except as the new rules could not argue with the various state's rules governing the first vote of each of their delegates be given according to the votes of the people in their states. With that caveat, therefore, anything could be changed aside from the nomination.

The rules committee, which rarely met prior to three days before said convention, called a quorum a month before and talked through their options that included, among others that

1. Acclimation be required for a nomination to be official and thus with Dyl's situation he could be stopped short and come what may;
2. At least two nominees exist for any nomination to be successful;
3. That no votes be counted from those involved with white supremacists, with avowed

communists, with racists, with misogynists, with those holding ties to LGBT antagonists, and so on;

4. That anyone with the first name Dylan couldn't be a nominee.

Of course, these are listed in priority order given that the last of them was impractical and devastating for the party given the state of minds of its base voters. The others remained in play as the meetings continued on into the wee hours of the night, day after day after day.

Thank God secrecy had been enforced so thoroughly that the committee, known to be meeting but about what other than reviewing the rules not known, were not allowed to leave the building in which they met. Or, for that matter, be given access to phones of any kind including their own cells.

35. Riots

Dylan, of course, found out about these secret meetings and pulled the plug on them. When, why, where, who, and what popped to the top of his agenda to discover and as he deliberated the possibility of real violence erupting in future stump speeches and wanting no part of it, he worked on the possibilities of phoning his presentations in. That is, to film them in advance and without letting audiences know which Dyl they would get, the real one or the virtual one.

Chaos ruled the day, something that Dyl loved and hated equally. Stumping for his party's efforts to invigorate the Congress with their own wasn't exactly something Dyl needed to do. No requirements in the party's book about that. So, without hesitation as was the case with most of Dylan's recent decisions, he cancelled his speaking tour and decided to take a vacation, at least for as long as he could stand it.

Meanwhile, the rules committee, knowing of his dropping out of said tour, discovered a new possibility that was the best of the now five under consideration. That being that Dylan Frye had never been a member of their party and could therefore not be that party's nominee no matter how many delegates he brought to the convention with him. This proved tricky to negotiate, but, given Dylan's pulling himself from support of the candidates in state races, he'd proven his lack of dedication to the party to which he'd associated himself with. That, plus the many anti-party points of view in the past over important critical issues, he'd erased his more or less paper trail. He'd given money to support rival candidates, he'd supported critical issues that the opposing party also supported, and, mostly, he'd never run for office on one of his declared party's ticket.

Of course, no one knew of the committee's tentative decision, and no one *would* know given that the committee who would guide the convention through its processes had decided to remain removed in their posh quarters in one of the buildings that, believe it or not, Dyl Frye owned. Their one final decision but yet to be finalized was who would be the party's nominee if not Dyl? How would this nominee, who had no delegates at this point, leap from non-entity to entity to nominee during a planned four-day convention filled almost entirely with delegates of one Dylan Frye?

During this time, Dyl had taken his family to Barbados to whoop it up with the ladies and the sun and the beaches and the booze and the ladies and the more ladies and the rest of it. Life was good, life was long, and life was boring, even with the ladies. After all, with his wife present, he could only look, not touch. So he worked on a new version of "Take back our country," the one that had grown old over the past weeks and that he thought might need refining before he got back into election mode.

Of course, Dyl knew that his replacement for Tom Benchley would be no help, and his long discussions with Gloria, his dog, had grown thin by this time. Whether he took the advice or not, having someone around, a yes-man, was better than not. He needed a Vice-President as well, better to select now on the sly than try to do it during the few days leading up to his nomination speech.

His choices for Vice President were so prolific that he seriously considered picking a name from a hat rather than taking the time necessary to give it to someone with designs on his own job. What he really needed was any old slacker wanting a position in the White House. No one was going to take the damn position with anything but alacrity, at least not when *Dyl* was alive. Of course, were something to happen to him, the job was next in line for his own and he couldn't not take that seriously.

So, he returned to the states and gave interviews to the most ept but least eager to be President. In other words, none of those who'd run against him in the primaries. He needed a personality contrasting his own since he didn't want competition. He also wanted someone who'd keep his nose out of anything salacious that Dyl might get himself involved in. Most importantly, he needed someone that could give good advice, but not take credit for it. This led to Tom, the first Tom, but Dyl knew the man would never take it. Nor give him advice on whom to choose.

A woman gave him pause. A perfect way to silence those who claimed him a sexist, but someone nagging him every day wouldn't do. So that was out. A black man might be the perfect thing to foil those who'd claimed him a racist, but, truth be known, he was a racist and it would likely make things worse. A white male it was, he had no choice. Except, of course, if the man were gay, and with that, he figured he could kill three birds with one stone, and no man who screwed men was going to stand up to the great and more than straight Frye.

His first interview was with a man by the name of Hawke. Ronald Hawke. A masculine sounding name, but someone completely out of the closet and already a state Senator with experience and no doubt chomping at the bit for a roll of high rank in the W.H. And in he came with his resume, dressed in the loudest suit Dyl had ever seen and speaking in the highest voice he'd heard only women use previously. Dyl bowed out immediately. No way could he take this creep for longer than a few minutes ne less for the eight years that he expected to be in office.

Age was about the only way he could figure it. Get the oldest, whitest male, straight as an arrow, and obsequious to the point of disgusting, and make sure he survived the eight years in office so the guy couldn't take over the helm. His very next interview, only this third so far, was the perfect fit. Almost eighty, nearly but not quite senile, able to walk but not without a cane, always with a smile on his face, and a white mustache to go with his mane of white hair. Married sixty years with six grown kids, and someone who really liked the way Dylan operated.

That was that. No big deal. Frye and Welkes. Thomas Welkes. A full-fledged lawyer with credentials and someone well liked in the Senate. A perfect fit and a member of his own party. And having the name Tom, sold it.

36. The Corps

While Dyl had thought he'd popped the cork on the rules committee meeting attempting to do him in during the convention, he hadn't come close to it. He found out as everyone else did, because someone on the committee could be bought and was, and the newspapers got hold of the information and published the whole sordid mess three weeks before the delegates arrived to listen to speeches and to vote for the presumptive sure thing.

Dyl was to be drummed out of the corps, the party itself, and thus become ineligible for becoming the party's nominee. The whole thing was brilliant, and, though Dyl had known of the possibility previously, he had no idea the committee would do it.

He needed his first Tom, or a first Tom fill in. Someone to give him advice when Dyl faced a firing squad by his own men. He also needed his fans to prop him back up on his pedestal. He'd gone far too long without them. Knowing first Tom wouldn't come back to work for him and not knowing anyone else as a substitute, Dylan charged ahead, created a major event with himself as the star, hired a whole bunch of Frye people as anti-Frye people to stir up a mess, provoked, or so it seemed but not so, by his party to categorically make Dyl appear unviable before the convention took place.

Twenty thousand people showed up, with half provided with signs that Dyl had decided should keep his original motto, "Take back our country," and the other half given signs that said, "Frye for Dog Catcher," a slogan that he'd originally thought would be, "Frye for Dog Fucker," but decided against it as being maybe a little over the top for primetime television, even the cable variety.

When he arrived and spoke, everything was so perfect. "This is soooo great. No, I mean it, soooo great. Unbelievable. Unbelievable. We love you. We really do. I mean it. Thousands of people here. So many you can't count them. Hundreds of thousands of people, I tell you. You know, you won't believe what's going on out there. You won't believe it. They're so freighted of how I'm going to take their little Washington apart, that they're saying that I can no longer be a part of their little party. Wooo, wooo. Their little party, and little it is, I can assure you. Little minds, little penises, and little women behind them. It's a downright tragedy. I say this with all due respect. I have lobbyists. I have to tell you they will do anything for me. Anything, I tell you. Anything. They're great. So, you know what? What my party is attempting to do, it won't happen. It won't happen. Won't happen. We want it to stop and it has to stop now. You hear me?"

With that, the two groups with different signs merged and the riots began. Staged yes, but not for long. Push someone without having instructions as to how hard and things can get out of hand quickly, and they did. Wooo, wooo.

The network cameras desperately tried to catch as much of the mess as they could. They'd already assumed that outside the convention center where the event had been scheduled, there would be a vast number of people who'd show up to watch and possibly join in the fun were that to happen. Some of these were anti-Frye folks, the real McCoy. Others paid to emulate the real ones by carrying the Frye-prepared signs, and, of course the pro-Frye folks with their signs. Then, though no one predicted this, unrelated gangs in the general area hearing of this clamored to get on board as fast as they could. This time, when Dyl claimed 'Hundreds of thousands of people' here abouts, he wasn't that far off base.

The cameras in the hall spun around and caught the beginnings of the uproar and the cameras outside caught the rest as the city of Mesa, Arizona outside of Phoenix, literally caught fire. The riot of riots had begun and would continue for days before the federal riot squads from the various protective agencies rushed in to stop the protests, brawls, anarchy, and chaos from destroying central Arizona.

Dylan, of course, was long gone by this time, hiding away in his penthouse in his LA tower and watching it unfold on TV.

Most importantly, the committee that had been revealed in the press and to which Dyl had delivered his response through the microphones at the convention center, were glued to their own TVs, aware now of the extent to which Dylan would take their decisions if they held true.

37. Stalemate

The stalemate between Dylan and the convention committee stood solid for a week before the committee designated to rid the party of their most hateful of candidates gave in and basically admitted to themselves that they, the most powerful of the powerful people in the party, had no way to do what they'd been required to do by the convention's highest and most dignified politicians in the country. Dylan ruled the day.

When Dyl got word of the change of mind well before the press did, he hugged Gloria, his dog, and screamed, "Victory at last," for everyone in the vicinity to hear. Loud and clear. For every intent and purpose, Dylan was already President of these United States and the only things left were his placing his hands on the Bible and telling everyone in the land that he, Dylan Frye, guaranteed that he would defend his country to his death, or whatever his response read that at that moment, he couldn't remember.

Since the opposing party held its convention early that year, Dyl got to watch and hear the most boring nomination he'd ever seen. No riots, no screams when the candidate spoke, no signs to show which candidate each delegate preferred since there was only one, and the word 'subdued' fit perfectly. Dyl worried that his nomination might turn out the same.

So he took the matter under advisement with his VP who gave him the only piece of sage advice he'd ever given to anyone. Anytime. Anywhere. That being to hold the process of voting to the shortest time possible and give the audience and viewers the wildest ride that he could in his acceptance speech. So enamored of this advice was Dylan that he stoked the fires by letting the press know in advance that they would hear the most rabble rousing and patriotic speech they'd ever heard. One that would have consequences heard round the world for decades to come. He guaranteed it would grace the textbooks of such things in schools for centuries to come and break the record for people watching at home. It was a large bear to enrage, but he did it. And come the day that everyone was in place in their seats or behind their cameras or with their pens poised, Dyl gave the speech of speeches, the spectacle of spectacles, the most loquacious and most garrulous of speeches ever given on earth.

"Ladies and gentlemen. I speak to you with great thanks in my heart for your unambiguous and gracious nomination of me as your candidate for President of these United States. I speak to those as well on television, radio, on the Internet, and in the trenches overseas helping to rid those who would attempt to destroy America. Our country has tremendous potentials. We have tremendous people. But we have been led by an administration without strength, without courage, and without stamina. As of this coming election that I will surely win, this will end. For us now, we will Take back our country."

Of course, the crowd roared, shoved their fists in the air several times, and made utter fools of themselves as expectations demanded.

"How stupid have our leaders been? These politicians. How idiotic are they? I'm going to tell you this. Now. Point to the so many ways they have betrayed us. They have given our jobs away to other countries. They've made arms deals with our enemies in exchange for nothing but words. They've begun wars that should never have begun. They've confused our friends. They've somehow betrayed those that depend on us. They've increased our national debt by trillions of dollars. They've created a supposedly universal health bill for Americans that costs much more than they can afford twofold over. They're letting the roads, railroads, bridges, airports, and many, many other things go to rot putting everyone at risk, I tell you. They're taking credit for lowering the jobless rate with most of the new jobs coming in at less than the minimum wage and claim they're improving the economy of America. They are not. No way. They're making it worse. Worse, I tell you, and this is only the beginning. I'm going to change these things. I can do it, I really can. You know it and I know it. Really I can. I'm not saying this to brag, because you know what? I don't have to brag. I don't have to, believe it or not. I'm saying that's the kind of thinking our country needs. We need that thinking. But we have the opposite thinking. We've been living under losers. The losers we mistakenly believe when we vote them into office. We have people that don't have it. Believe me. They don't have it. They are selling this country down the drain."

Dylan took a deep breath and listened to the applause, the screams, the yells, and the kisses thrown at him from everywhere in the country, from both parties. He wasn't reading from a script or a teleprompter. This was coming from Dylan's brain as he spoke the words. From the heart. Of course, saying these things didn't mean a thing, but he had that Frye charisma. No question about it. The man was a perfect example of a flimflam artist.

"Now, let me get down to specifics. What am I going to do so you'll know I mean business? First and foremost, every leader in this world, the minute I take office, is going to know that things have changed as far as we are concerned. There's a new kid on the block and he's going to turn things around. He's operating from a point of strength and they're going to pay attention and learn from him. Or else. Second we're getting those jobs back. No more trade agreements where we lose jobs or lose money. I'll tax the bunch of them, our companies, so much so they'll have to go bankrupt to stay alive or bring their jobs back home. We're going to work on our roads, trains, bridges, and airports to make them right. More jobs, see? We're going to stop making wars and fix them. Any we have to make, we're going to win them but quick. No more pussyfooting around. We're going to build our military, fund them appropriately, and take care of our vets. On and on. The minute I'm in office we're going to make anyone who wants to be a part of the U.S. of A. work their asses off for the privilege. Yes.

I mean it. Those who are here that would attempt to destroy us will be found and themselves destroyed. No more games I tell you. This is for real. We're going to work from a position of strength from now on."

The audience roared some more. Even those in their homes had sat up and were, no doubt, reciting or singing "Take Back Our Country." Dyl knew it. The live audience knew it. The news people knew it. No more shitting around, this was the real deal. Not the new deal, but the real deal.

"You've heard others talk about these things. Talkers. My competitors. Just talk, I say. With me you get the real thing. Strength. This country will no longer play with toys, but the real things. The real deal."

Boy did he like that phrase. Not the 'new deal' of Roosevelt, but the 'real deal' of Dylan Frye. He reminded himself to make that another of his oft repeated quotes for the press. "Take Back Our Country," and "The Real Deal." Because it *was* the 'real deal.' Absolutely.

The cheers kept coming. He could go on for the rest of the night without stopping, but he didn't want to wear them out.

"Let me finish with a thought that might make you stand up and salute the flag. America is not only the best country in the world, it is the hope of the world. Maybe the last hope. This hope that we represent is a perfect hope that strength and honor will forever continue in our name. Be proud of your country. Our best times are ahead. We will persevere. I guarantee it. We will persevere. Together. Now, with me, let's put our hands over our hearts and Pledge our Allegiance to the Flag for which it Stands."

The live audience did as told. Of course they did. Wouldn't you?

38. Positive Critics

The next-day editions of the major newspapers in the country headlined Dyl's acceptance speech at the convention. Most were positive, some extremely so, and a rare negative here and there.

The Times read, "Frye's presentation was flawless, Presidential, and didn't waste a single word. He covered everyone of the major issues and stated his opinion from a position of strength in a clear and unambiguous way." This coming from his most severe of critics.

The Post went further, saying, "One of the best acceptance speeches this reporter has ever heard. Covered everything from A to Z and clarified any question that anyone might have. The audience in attendance and that at home could easily be heard cheering him on. Without a doubt Frye cemented himself as the front runner as we enter the last lap of the Presidential race."

The LA papers gave him credit. Mostly because Hollywood had never seen an improvised on the spot speech delivered in such a powerful yet relaxed way.

Clearly, Dyl was on his way to the White House with only himself to blame if he didn't get there.

Then, one day and most certainly out of the blue, one day after the speech, Tom Benchley appeared at Dylan's penthouse door.

"Tom?"

"Dyl."

"What brings you up my way?"

"Caught your acceptance speech the other night."

"So, what did you think?"

"Like everyone else, it was brilliant. I'm wondering if you'd take me back."

All this happening within a minute caught Dylan completely by surprise.

"Why? If my speech was so good, why would I need you?"

"Good question."

"You have a good answer?"

"Yes. Read this."

Tom handed Dyl the front page of the Chicago Tribune.

"Yeah, I read it. Didn't find it very interesting."

"I'm sure you didn't. But you have to take everything seriously. Reporters have different degrees of competency. I happen to know this one. He's brilliant."

"Yeah?"

"Yeah."

"You want me to read it again?"

"Yes. Or at least tell me why you didn't find it interesting."

"Because it found fault with me about stuff I never said in the speech."

"You're right. He found fault with you for making statements that to a fault contradicted statements you'd made in the past. Makes you look like someone who flips your take on important issues to get votes, not based on principles."

"He says I'm a schizophrenic. That I have six different personalities for God's sake."

"Probably more than that, Dyl. But we have problems. You broadcast yours. Instructive criticism, I'd say."

"I thought the phrase was 'constructive criticism.'"

"It is, but in your case, and if you hire me back, it can be instructive criticism."

"So you want to come back so you can explain to me my own personality?"

"No. I want to come back to keep one of those personalities at the forefront and send the others to backstories. You're so close. So right on so many issues. But tomorrow you could go somewhere and blow everything you've gained. That saddens me. So close, and yet so far."

"Same salary?"

"Less if you need the money."

"You think I need money, Tom?"

"No."

"The same salary it is. Welcome home, buddy."

So it was that Tom Benchley rejoined the Dylan Frye team again, attempting to keep Dyl on the straight and narrow without realizing it or, apparently, remembering that such an ordeal would be impossible. Maybe, however, he could minimize the damage and keep the public from remembering that once elected, his boss was a hand's length from the red phone that would set the world afire and the planet into self-destruct mode.

The establishment of his party had given up. With that speech under his belt, Dylan was once again in full-speed-ahead mode with his party fully supporting him for the rest of the way. Everyone saw the path to the White House and if Dylan Frye didn't self-destruct along the way somehow, they'd be in sole power of the Washington elite for many years to come with promising continuance in store for the future.

Dylan, though, was Dylan, and steel chains couldn't keep him from veering from his appointed rounds and keep his damn mouth shut after he had everything basically wrapped up. One negative word against him by anyone, anywhere, provoked one of his alternate personalities to rear its ugly head and he'd become the famed loose cannon, his own worst enemy, and causing Tom, the party, or the press to force him into defensive mode.

Someone in the press, for example, might call him a warmonger and he'd take it personally, saying, "War? You think I'm a warmonger? Well, buddy, you ain't seen nothin' yet." And out would pour threats to every country who'd expressed a view on the subject reminding them of the arsenal of nukes he would have at his disposal. Readers would quickly realize that they'd heard a particular version of Dyl the night of his acceptance, and he could easily shift to another mode and create war with a friendly neighbor, no less an enemy.

But Tom had been ready for this, chastising Dyl while putting out fires as quickly as they caught on. As he now remembered so vividly, keeping up with

Dylan was like attempting to race a cheetah in Africa. You could shovel his droppings but not prevent him from beating you at his game.

Tom made Dyl bring Gloria into the office with him since the dog seemed to have a certain calming effect on the man. He also pre-read the newspapers and clippings before Dylan got to see them to avoid mishaps. But the Internet and television cable shows made up for that. Dyl proved tireless as he always had, sleeping maybe three hours a night, and those three hours mostly in-between angry spots of waking hours tweeting the world and starting feuds that had begun like love letters. He hired someone to keep tabs on Dyl when Tom had to sleep with express orders for the man to wake him whenever Dyl sent out insults on his private computer.

Riots had calmed since the convention and Dylan got into the mode to repeating himself over and over again. A good thing for his staff. A bad thing for his campaign. But Dyl had such a lead at this time that one point here or there made little difference.

But next came the Presidential Debates. Two only since Dyl's opponent had argued for the fewer the better since, as everyone knew, Frye would annihilate the poor man whenever on stage at the same time. Dyl had seen to that by knocking off his opponent's opponents.

39. Whistle Stop

Everything ran smoothly. Tom had come back, three months left before the general, Dyl's challenger had to make up twenty points in the polls before breaking even no less going ahead, and nothing would break Dyl's momentum. Except, of course, Dyl. That was it. Dyl could do it and would if Tom couldn't stop him first. Both men knew it as well. Tom because of his experience, and Dyl due to his increasing boredom with Gloria to sooth the savage beast. Dylan.

Tom scheduled a whistle stop tour across America. One of those where speeches were made from the rears of trains and crowds contained by stations and reluctance of local police concerned about bad reflections on their communities because of the famed Dylan riots. A perfect way to handle things. Control the variables as best you could.

Dyl, of course, hated the whole idea. He wanted to stay in one or another of his penthouse suites, not on the restrictive moving bedrooms of the best of Amtrack's offerings. But Tom prevailed and the three-week trip organized. Across the northern rustbelt states, on to the Midwest farmers, into the mountains of Wyoming, Montana, and stopping briefly in Seattle. Then down the coast to San Francisco and onto LA, where the return trip would cover the more southern routes and catching up with Saint Louis, Cincinnati and down to Florida including Texas and Louisiana along the way. Finally up the eastern seaboard and to the Big Apple. Lots of scenery to see with barely a half hour to get Dyl into trouble twice a day from the back of a caboose, one of those old jobs fitted especially for a more modern rear of a more modern express.

Wife number three, Katrina, K, came along for the ride this time to keep Dylan sated enough so he wouldn't leap into the fog and forget where he was or what he was saying. Or attempt to make pals with the few press accompanying the entourage and give up some privileged secrets for the newspapers to print.

For the first few days, everything went—as they say—swimmingly. Dyl kept to his vaguely scripted speeches, enjoyed being out of doors, and the hearing of the marching bands playing "Take Back Our Country." But he tired of the routine and one of his apparently multiple personalities came rushing to the rescue and out came what the press had come for and were willing and able to phone back to the home desks.

"No one gets the better of Dylan Frye," he said, for no apparent reason and no apparent target. Out of the blue because he felt like saying it.

"Strength is my middle name, I tell you. No, I mean it." The crowd noticed his change of speech pattern. The angrier his temper, the more he devolved into his earlier form of speaking.

"I'll nuke 'em, I tell you. I'll nuke 'em." Then something popped in Dyl's brain and for the first time Tom and Katrina noticed the sudden changes in character. Into and out of it without any advanced warning.

The crowd of farmers, though, loved it and applauded wildly. Dyl smiled at this, forgetting that the press was everywhere and that local cameras were recording him for YouTube showings that would likely go viral.

The word 'nuke' had opposite effects on those living in the country and those in cities. For farmers and ranchers, the endless country they could see around them gave them the security of knowing that any incoming nukes would likely fall into the open spaces with few killed. The city folks knew the opposite. Everyone in high rises and jammed into the streets gave promise that a 'nuke' would likely kill tens of thousands if not millions. To a true politician who knows his stuff, never say the word 'nuke' no matter where you are. The word was as dangerous to say as it was to see exploding in front of your eyes.

There, Dyl had said it. Had threatened it. As if 'nuking' a country wouldn't create return fire and that many of those watching and reading about his speech that day wouldn't survive his threat. The very reason he himself had eliminated the word from his acceptance speech. No nukes anywhere in it. But he'd invited it back into the discussion this very day on the train and it would follow him now wherever he went.

Tom was irate. Mad as a hatter. For the first few minutes with Dyl, Tom was less in control than he'd been as he stood against the rails of the caboose that morning.

"You idiot," he yelled. "You fucking idiot. How could stand out there and mess everything you yourself set up at the convention. For God's sake, we'll be taking this back until the election. The reporter in Chicago or wherever was right about you. You're a loose cannon of loose cannons. Six personalities, hell, you have twenty, with never any way to tell which one's going to appear at any given moment. What made you do that, huh? What?"

"Seemed like the right thing to say," Dyl replied.

"But you see now, don't you, that it wasn't the right thing to say?"

"I guess. But it'll go away. Like the things I said before I gave that now famous speech went away. You'll see."

But 'nuke' didn't go away. Not in the least. It stuck around and stuck around like Gloria did, sniffing at Dyl's heels and peeing on his pants' legs every chance it got. Biting like one of snakes-for-hair on Medusa's head. Randomly coming from nowhere and at any time it felt the need.

40. Death in Venice

But it didn't go away, instead it got worse. Not exactly 'it,' but his campaign that couldn't be stopped but spent more of its time sputtering. The VP died suddenly. Not that it was that unexpected, but that the timing was off. Way off. Between terms would have worked best. Four years later maybe. Or after Dyl's presumptive eight years was over. Not before they'd begun.

Now, Dylan not only had to quell rumors that he may be losing his mind due to his stumble on the nukes thing, but he had to replace the VP between his nomination and the election. All from a moving train on its way to LA.

The powers that be, noticing the way in which Dylan would be fine for a month or two and then strike a match in a dynamite factory got an idea that would add fuel to Dylan's self-induced fires by considering that the delegates had agreed to support the two men, P and VP, not only P, and now, before taking office, only the P remained, and that that meant that they might have one last opportunity to knock P off. It was a long shot to be sure, especially since they had pretty much of a lock on grabbing the Senate and the house as well as the presidency, but they were also Americans, who like the rest of us worried about nukes dropping and exploding in their backyards.

From the top of the mountain, Dylan dropped to near bottom once again. He desperately needed to

right the ship and was ready to take Tom's advice no
matter how difficult it may be to swallow the
seawater, no matter how hard that terribly struggled
metaphor was to waddle through.

So, the two of them met behind locked doors
and Tom talked and Dyl listened. As impossible as
that may sound.

"All we need is three things, Dyl. Three little
things. Then we're back to normal again. Three things.
Are you ready for me to tell you what these three
things are?"

Dylan nodded rather than spoke.

"Good. First, you've got to guarantee yourself,
not so much me but me too, that you will never, ever,
ever again go off script like you did back their.
Understand?"

Dylan nodded again.

"Second, we find another patsy, a much, very
much younger patsy for VP and push him the hell
through the establishment before we have to get
Congress to affirm him. Understand?"

Dylan nodded yet again.

"Finally we need you to apologize for what you
said without sounding weak or telegraphing that
you'll never drop a nuke on another country when in
fact you might, God forbid, have to when you're in
office."

"How do I do that?"

"I'll write the thing and we'll begin with it in
your LA speech and leave the damn problem alone for
once and forever. That's not too much to ask is it?"

"No," Dylan said, "depending on what you write, of course."

"Of course,"

"What are you going to write?"

"Don't know yet. But it will, you can be guarantied, be short and sweet."

"My kind of apology," Dylan said.

"Mine, too," Tom added.

The next morning, Tom came into Dyl's sleeper after knocking to make sure he was up and not busy with something else.

"Here it is. I think you'll be pleased," Tom said.

Dyl read it. "This is it?"

"Yep."

"Wow. This is perfect. 'Apparently my comments recently have been misinterpreted by some to mean I felt calm about using certain types of explosives on countries that oppose us. I don't feel comfortable. At the same time if intelligence sources confirm that a power that be is imminently going to annihilate us, I will not hesitate to make sure that doesn't happen. I hope that clarifies this misunderstanding and calms those confused.'"

"You should say it calmly and without emotion and get right on with your presentation to avoid questions that might invite more confusion. Got it?"

"Absolutely."

"Here's your VP."

Dyl read the sheet quickly.

"Wilkes Booth? That rings a bell."

"Should. It was John Wilkes Booth that assassinated Lincoln."

"Why him? Especially with that name?"

"He's sixty, a centrist, quiet, respected, and, except for his name, mostly unknown to the general public. Perfect."

"He won't assassinate me?"

"Nope. Good family man with an extended family."

"Meaning?"

"Four kids, and four grandchildren."

"Fine with me. If he'll stay out of the way."

"He will. Meet with him and you'll see."

"Okay. When?"

"He'll join our assembly in LA before you speak and come with us back to Washington."

"I look forward to it. Tom, you're a gem."

"I know it and you know it. But let's keep that between us, okay?"

"Sure," Dyl said, slightly confused as to why Tom had put it that way.

41. Quelling Doubts

Between stops, the party contacted Dyl to inform him that his selection of a VP must pass their standards as well as his and that once he selected someone to make no announcements before they'd okay'd it.

None of this made Dylan any too happy, but he guessed that some hidden rules or past conventions should be followed and agreed, hoping that Tom's choice and Dyl's speech in LA would quell any doubts they had over his choice.

The minute the train entered north LA, that being San Fernando Valley for those unfamiliar with the area, every thought of things blowing away in a quiet wind disappeared. Not strangely enough for those who knew the area better than Dyl, students of the hundreds of colleges and universities in the area had illegally gathered in certain areas to block the train's progress and police warned that Amtrack needed to stop the train until peace could be restored. And back into the soup Dyl's campaign went, like sliding down a steep hill covered in ice.

'What else could a no more than two-minute aberration during a whistle stop in the prairie cause?' Dylan thought, and took one of his pills to calm him down. Not the sleeping kind, but the ones that targeted his dopamine center to make it provide him the natural high that ne needed at the moment.

"Great," Tom yelled as he came running into Tom's room, this time without knocking. We've got thousands of young people out there ready and waiting for you to talk to them."

"Out there? Outside the train? Here?"

"No, but at certain stops along the say. We're going to set the cops up with loudspeakers and you'll give your speech here inside the train and they'll play it at those locations."

"Why is this great?"

"Because, Dyl, this is a demographic that we're missing right now. We don't really need their votes I don't think, but having them will double our guarantee of winning by a landslide in two weeks."

"Sounds good."

"Right. Let's get you in the right space and have you tape the speech and I think you'll find that what a few minutes ago sounded like a disaster, isn't anymore."

Meantime, the two debates set between Dyl and his other party competition were set close together, after the whistle stop train tour and the November day of the election. The two candidate staffs had settled on two two-hour slots on different cable news networks hosted by well-known moderators selected by each network based on their own contrasting biases. While Dyl's far behind campaign staff rehearsed him daily for the two-hour grind, Dyl spent his time trying to convince Tom that he wouldn't go off script again and embarrass his chances of the too obvious landslide that was about to occur in his favor.

Both debates looked on paper like boring boxing matches with both candidates on the defensive and trying to not do something rather than doing something.

When Dyl shook his opponent's hand on stage before the first question, his almost crushing grip caused the man to visibly wince and they were off to the races. First questions were too simple and without anything one could say in response that would be untoward. Like blending coffee with watermelons. Or more like, "Which candidate has given you the most trouble so far?" or "On what basis did you select your vice President?" or "Which party do you think will win the house and the Senate?" 'No one,' 'perfect for the job,' and 'we'll carry both thank you very much,' were the right answers and both got them correct.

The second brace of questions proved more difficult, like, "How will you pay for your promised this or that?" or "Do you believe in trickle down or fountain economics?" or "How do you plan to pay for this whatchamacallit that you've promised the people in your campaign?" and so on. The answers became more complicated and more volatile when their answers invited follow up questions.

But Dyl's opponent remained as aloof as he could and didn't bite when the moderator attempted to ignite fights between the two of them. Dyl followed suit. Tom, watching on his home television set smiled as his man kept the peace and did not make a mistake, as if he'd seen the questions in advance which Tom was sure he hadn't.

When the first debate finished and the pundits called it a boring draw with nothing being revealed from either side, Dyl confronted Tom to argue that these things were worthless and for the second one he had to be let off his leash. He'd go crazy if he left it alone and didn't get his way. Tom worked for him and Dyl could do anything he wanted. What he wanted would prevail second time around.

42. Debating

By the time the second debate rolled around and unbeknownst to Tom, something in Dyl had pulled a chain and loosed his tongue. For the first question brought immediate reaction. Dyl's inner web had always been there, but the spiders had hidden since Tom had returned and now they'd come out to bite for real.

The question posed went something like this, "Is the Second Amendment helping to arm the crazies out there to commit their heinous crimes? What would you do to curtail guns if you agree?"

The question had been asked of Dylan's opponent, but he didn't get a chance to answer. Dyl jumped in before he had a chance.

"No, dammit, no. We need more guns, not less. At one time I was against guns. I didn't want guns. But now I see the error of my ways. We should have guns, guns, guns. Everywhere guns. In our closets, in our bedrooms, kitchens, on our tables. Everywhere. We need more guns, not less. We should teach our kids about guns, have guns in the schools. None of these mass shootings of kids would occur if these nutcases knew that instead of defenseless kids they'd come up against armed commandos. Guns, I say. It's how we created this great country and how we'll return it to its greatness. I say, 'Take back our country.'"

Tom, sitting in the green room, went ballistic. Not only had Dylan swore on national television, not only had he stolen a question away from his opponent, but he'd taken a radical stance on one of the most hot-button issues of the day. This was going to be one hell of a ride, and it had just begun.

Yet, the crowd in attendance, a carefully chosen crowd to make sure one candidate or the other didn't get an unfair advantage, went crazy. The applause wouldn't stop. Tom went numb. What did this mean? Dyl and he had gone through a lot together. Had his real self returned and it turned out to be what the public actually wanted?

The moderator, after making sure the candidate on the other side of the aisle had a chance to put his two cents in, and that was what it was worth, two cents, a kind of middle of the road non-answer, hadn't prepared a follow-up question since it was assumed the two candidates would dance around the issue. So he improvised with, "How would you propose to do this?"

Of course this question was aimed at Dylan who by now had garnered the attention of the audience, the cameras, and the other candidate. So Dyl took it with amazing grace.

"I would rewrite the Second Amendment to state that not only shall everyone have as many guns of as many types as possible without any checks, background or otherwise, but that they may brandish them at will. More importantly, I would have that amendment state that no other amendment may amend this new version for the end of time."

The audience lost it completely providing not only continuing applause but a standing ovation taking so long that some of the television coverage took several commercial breaks and made some money during the near half hour response to Dylan's take on the matter.

Tom had bent himself into a fetal position at this point, afraid to look at the monitor and see the fights which no doubt would start soon, though none did, and fearful again that his candidate Dylan Frye would win the election and become President, a thought that now brought chills to him.

The Wild Dyl would return the minute any such amending of the Amendment would occur. Citizens of our fair country would turn it into a catastrophic nightmare, with death-by-gunshot becoming a daily occurrence even in the smallest of towns. He could see twelve-year olds dueling in the streets and mad drivers on freeways shooting anyone who got in their way. Housewives would have assault weapons ready for their husbands' first cross words. He had feared the 'nuke' business would put Dylan in hot water and had been right. This guns for everyone would put him in office for life apparently.

When things calmed down, the moderator forgot to ask the question to Dyl's combatant and the debate went south from there, with every question giving Dylan a chance to up the ante of the previous one with a greater opportunity to drive the audience in attendance to further hysterics. Nukes came up and the audience broke into chanting, "Take back our country." "Take back our country."

Tom didn't wait around to pick up the pieces, he left the building and hiked to the nearest bar, figuring the exact wording of his resignation as he did. Either way the election went, he wanted no part of it. A weasel and a psychopath as choices, the country was going down in flames either way. He planned his route to northern Canada to escape his career and hopefully the fall of the greatest country on earth. Hannibal and his elephants had arrived and the empire ready to succumb to the barbarians.

Dyl, on the other hand, when the debate ended, clasped his opponent's hand and vigorously shook it. To him, Dylan that is, everything had gone swimmingly. Once again he was king of the hill. Everyone loved him and he loved every one of them in return. Life was good. Hell, life was great.

Katrina was the first to congratulate him. She'd been born long after WWII and had been raised in aristocracy. What did she know of violence and bombs, and munitions and all the other things? She, like the audience, felt that her husband was a hero. A great man. Someone who would empower America with guts and bravery so that the world would shutter with fear in response to his strength and power and threats to their existence if they didn't behave. Dylan was in heaven, of course. He had no idea how Tom felt about his performance, but didn't really care. The people loved him again, and loving and being loved was the center of his universe. So everything was well in Dyl World.

The moderator collapsed and went into shock after witnessing what he'd thought would be a simple and final debate between two intellectuals but had instead fallen through a trapdoor leaving him as the scapegoat.

43. Opposing Views

Interestingly, the newspaper editors and the talking heads on television took strangely opposite views to those regular citizens who had witnessed the clobbering of a defenseless opponent by Dylan and the onslaught of Dyl's opinions. He couldn't understand the disparity. It pissed him off. It drove him nuts. Tom had disappeared without a word said, and Dyl was lost in this unexpected negative reaction to what he'd done. Those were his real views, weren't they?

So, in short, Dylan Frye was, apparently, back on his own, a man ready to finish off the one who would be king instead of him. He knew exactly how to do it. Accusations of infidelity. It might be a hard sell given that his opponent had the testicles of a timid squirrel, but it would also be the last straw. Good grief, the man wrote poetry. Poetry, for God's sake. Dyl, at least in his mind, could exhale hard and blow the man down.

So he called the Times and the Post and anonymously claimed that his opponent had two ladies in waiting at his beck and call and was taking great sexual liberties with them, liberties so out of bounds that he, the anonymous caller, couldn't imagine stating to the press or anyone else for that matter, what, in fact, they did once alone together. Then, disguising his voice again and this time giving them a false name as a source, reiterated the claims and promised to bring in photographs to make the accusations stick.

For this project, Dyl wanted the very best photo touchup artist in the world. Therefore, he needed a single photograph with the candidate and the two girls performing some kind of outrageous sexual shenanigans, the more impossible to believe the better, but a photograph that could not be reversed engineered in any way. A perfect job that couldn't be proven fake.

In short, he needed Tom. Not to create the retouched photo, but to find the right man to do it. Dyl had no experience at such things nor did any of his other staff still with him. So, he put his brain to work in finding Tom and bringing him back into the fold. Tom had not resigned and no matter where he was, how far away or how distant in temperament at this point, getting him back on board was of highest priority.

He found him, of course. In northern Canada on a lake that fortunately had frozen over for the upcoming winter and therefore not good for fishing at the moment, and he brought him back to the states and into his eagerly waiting arms.

"I quit," Tom said, before Dyl had an opportunity to welcome him back.

"We need you, Thomas," Dyl told him, using his formal name to indicate how serious he was.

"Not going to do it. Not going to watch you implode again."

"I have a bigger lead than ever."

"See. So you don't need me."

"But I do."

"Why?"

"To keep things on a stable keel. To keep us going in the right direction. To win the election. Can't do it without you, buddy."

"You're doing it right by yourself."

"No way. A lucky guess on my part."

"What is it you *really* need, Dyl?"

"So many things, Tom, so many things."

"Right this minute, I mean."

"Right this minute, I need you to find someone who can professionally hack photographs. Someone so good that the end product won't give a trace that it's a fake."

At that second, Tom made a break for the door. Dyl's staff, however, had prepared for this moment and brought him back and sat him down again.

"Are you kidnapping me, Dyl?"

"No, Tom. I'm going to increase your salary to double what it was."

"Not worth it."

"It will be when you hear what it's for."

"I can guess that."

"You can?"

"Yes. A photo with naked ladies involving your competition for Election Day."

"How'd you know?"

"The exact kind of dirty trick I would expect of you, Dyl. This other you, I mean. A month ago you wouldn't even have thought of such a thing. But you've regressed for some reason, back into the power thing. I don't know what did it, but you're back and I want no part of it."

"Hang on, Tom, will you?"

"No."

"You have to, Tom. You didn't actually quit, you know, and I won't fire you. I won't accept your resignation. You work for me. Still. So this little thing? I won't ask anything more of you that you don't want to do."

"A name is what you want?"

"Yes."

"Barton Rascal."

"You made that up."

"No, seriously. That's his name. He's the best."

"You know him?"

"Yes, a long time ago. But we didn't leave on shall I say good terms, so if you're thinking of asking me to ask him on this forget it. Won't work. You'll have to ask him yourself. Or have one of your other staff do it. I won't. Oh, and by the way, I resign. I'm gone. No more of this shit, Dyl. I've had it. I really have."

"Write down the details for my staff and I'll let you go."

"You will? Really?"

"Yes, really."

Tom stared at Dyl for a time, not believing what he was hearing, and a grimace creased his lips.

"I don't have any money on me. You were in too much of a hurry. I can't go anyplace."

"Stay here until the election and you'll be going back to Canada in luxury, Tom. Luxury. Buy the place where you stayed instead of paying rent. Enjoy life. Just a little over a week to go. That's it. A week, Tom. I don't have any other tricks up my sleeve."

"Sleeves, Dyl, sleeves."

"Sleeves. Will you do it?"

"Can't give me a small loan?"

"Not on your life."

"The King of Crap strikes again, huh?"

"Amazing, am I not?"

"Not the word I'd use, but okay. Until the day after the election. Win or lose. And not inauguration day either. One week from tomorrow."

"Deal."

"Deal."

Tom made the call and within forty-eight hours the deed was done. Every paper in the country had headlines with a retouched copy of the photo leaving out the private parts of the various *ménage à trois* positions taken. The tabloids had it first, following that the mainstream press, and following that the cable networks. Of course, the Internet beat everyone to the punch and the photo absolutely went viral, but for some reason that didn't count in the same way as traditional media.

Thus, it took less than ten minutes for Dyl's staff to spread the bogus photo and rumors abounded and caught on. Unfortunately, a little over twenty-four hours later they pulled the plug on the forgery. But damage is damage and once accused, never forgotten. So the absentee ballots from those hours and the memories gained had been worth the effort, and Dylan had gained the upper hand on his opponent.

44. Return

Tom was back in the fold, if only until the election proper. But Dylan immediately found himself in another crises for which Thomas could not bail him out. His real estate business, a major source of his self-funding upon which he prided himself, had gone under in the recession that now blanketed the western world. Bankruptcy presented the only way out, but declaring a Chapter 7 at this point in time would be virtual suicide for the Frye campaign. He needed to stall things somehow. But how, exactly?

In short, Dylan Frye, the billionaire, needed money, and needed it fast, or else everything he now enjoyed would vanish, and the man who would be king would crumble into the man who was a pauper. Not something any of his voters and potential voters wanted to hear.

This translated to bribes, borrowing, theft, delays, and unkept promises. There were likely other ways to go, but in this short time—and his creditors were insistent on immediacy—he could think of nothing else. Bribes, theft, delays, and promises seemed doubtful, leaving only borrowing as the faint but possible alternative. But there things got worse rather than better. While he might get a loan, what would keep the loaner from breaking the news before the election? He had to find someone capable of lending him a large sum of money for a short period of time on a minute's notice whom he could trust. Absolutely trust.

Back to Tom, who could be trusted because he still thought the opposing candidate would be a worse choice than Dyl and who no doubt knew people of rich resources.

"But I don't," Tom said when asked.

"You don't know anyone like that?"

"That can bail you out of a bankruptcy of what, twenty million smackers? No way. Why would you think that, Dyl?"

"Because I've seen you when we're out on the stump. You schmooze with the best of them."

"Not the same. I'm not asking them for money."

"Yeah, but they'd probably say yes if you did, wouldn't they?"

"No. Really, you're asking the wrong guy, Dyl."

"Well try this. Is there someone you know who knows someone who'd be willing to lend me the money for a few weeks or so?"

"Aside from someone that works for the mob, you mean?"

"Yeah. Not the mob."

"No, I don't."

"What am I going to do?"

"Sell one or more of your buildings. That should do it. You have the money just not in liquid form."

"That would do it, but I can't do that in a week."

"Use the down payment on a sale, wouldn't that work?"

"Nice try, but no. Selling something that fast would be as bad as selling nothing. I'd take a loss so big that in the end I'd still be up for bankruptcy."

"So it's in the timing?"

"Yes."

"Humm."

"Is that humm for maybe there's someone you know, or humm you think you might be able to embezzle it?"

"Not sure. Let me think about it for a minute."

"Right."

Tom crawled into his own brain and Dyl sat back and tried to think of something, anything that would take his mind off spending the rest of his life peddling popcorn on a street corner.

"You could try Wilkes Booth."

"Huh? My Vice President nominee."

Right."

"He rich?"

"Not particularly, but he owns a home in upstate New York that's worth millions. His family willed it to him and he's kept it up beautifully."

"Worth?"

"At least twenty million. It's on about two hundred acres of pristine vineyards, some of the best wines the state has to offer. You've never heard of Booth's Best?"

"I have, but didn't know that was his brand."

"Is."

"You think he'd loan me the bread for a month or so?"

"I do. If this gets out, he'll lose the election as well as you. He's got as much to loose as you do, therefore."

"Could you ask him for me?"

"No way. You ask him. I'm your campaign manager, not your beggar."

"Wilkes?"

"Dylan. What's up?"

"I've got a personal question to ask you. Could you come by my office for an hour or so?"

"Sure, when?"

"Now would be good."

"I'll be there in ten minutes."

"Perfect."

With the doors and windows closed, the two of them facing one another, Dylan explained his problem to Wilkes as well as he could under the circumstances.

"My company doesn't have the cash on hand to pay the workers in my various hotels and casinos. So I either have to go the Chapter 7 route and declare bankruptcy which, as you no doubt can guess, will likely put us back into our civilian jobs not in the White House, or find someone willing to loan me enough to make it over this rough spot."

"You think I can do this?"

"Yes."

"How much we talking about?"

"Twenty million will do it."

"For how long?"

First hurdle over, Dyl thought.

"A month or two at most."

"What about interest?"

"You'll get back whatever the bank asks for."

"Done."

"What?"

"Consider it done. I'll set it up later this afternoon and you'll have the money in your account by tonight."

"You can do this, Wilkes?"

"I can do this, Dylan. I'm going to do it."

He did.

45. The Tightening Polls

The race was on. Days to go and the polls still had it tight. Wasn't possible, but his rival had somehow pulled even and maybe a point or two over. Too close to call. So Dylan called upon his family to join him in his final speeches in important states to hopefully add the homespun touch to his last minute begging.

Unlikely that after so many victories along the way, he wasn't still miles ahead of his nemeses, but he wasn't. As the days passed and so the hours, Dyl developed a good case of laryngitis during which he squeaked rather than squawked and, as was Tom's preference, barely talked letting his sons do it for him.

But the polls pulled closer yet as if that were possible. A dead heat. A tie in the making. All this, of course, based on the head count, not by state, in other words the overall vote across the country. Those in the know, however, realized that voters vote for electors who represent their states in the electoral college and that those votes decide who wins the election, not the mass votes that really don't amount to anything except affecting the electors. Regular votes tallied not by state but for the country at large are obviously important and both candidates knew that. But, in order that one highly populated area of major cities in the east, for example, won't have complete control over who wins that tally of votes, the electoral college, not a college really but a group of people who meet and vote for their candidate required by their respective states, really decides the matter. Bush versus Gore in 2000 represents a case in point, with Gore winning the popular vote and Bush winning the electoral college vote and thus becoming President. Doesn't seem logical or possible, but there it is.

Dylan, based on the polls taken in fifty states, understood this with Tom, of course, giving him the details. Each state had a number of electors based on their number of Senators, two, and their number of representatives, whatever, with a winner take all in every one but two states. What Tom told him didn't look good. While close, Dyl's opponent came out seven electoral votes ahead of Dylan in almost every way you took it. No matter Dyl's popular vote tallies, he was heading toward a loss that Tom, with his reservations about Dyl's sanity, found eminently depressing.

"We've got to do something, Tom. I'm going to lose though I've won? We've got to do something, Tom."

"Not much we can do, Dyl. It is what it is."

"I know you think I'm a flibbertigibbet, Tom, but there must be something we can do."

"A what?"

"What?"

"That thing you said I thought you were."

"A flibbertigibbet?"

"Yeah, that."

"A whack job, Tom. A nutcase. That kind of thing."

"How'd you ever learn that word?"

"You never seen the film 'Joe Versus the Volcano?' Tom Hanks and Meg Ryan who plays several roles and calls herself a flibbertigibbet in one of them. Great film, you should see it."

"Right. What were we talking about?"

"I think we were talking about the election, Tom. You were telling me I was going to lose and that it was what it was."

"Oh, yeah."

"Any ideas?"

"Only one."

"What?"

"Cheat."

Dyl stared at Tom for a second, realizing that he didn't mean it, but that maybe the hullabaloo of getting this far and missing the target had gotten to him as well and that he did mean it.

"Okay. How?"

"Easy. Find a state that's really close with at least seven electors. That state will have to use computers to count the votes. Sue the state once the final tally's in, and get a hacker to switch the count from your opponent to you. Hope he doesn't get caught and you're in. You win by seven rather than him. See how it works?"

"I think I do."

"You could do it with a really small state with, say only four votes. That'll reduce his tally by four to three lead and up your tally to four instead and you'd win the Electoral College by one vote."

"Where do I get a hacker to do this that won't talk?"

"Hell, half the twelve year olds in the country could do it and certainly would do it if the pay was good enough and you could convince them that it was an experiment. No harm no foul. As smart as those little people are at some things like computers, they don't know shit about politics."

"How much pay?"

"Maybe a hundred bucks. Maybe a little less depending on the kid."

"That's it?"

"Well we have to pick a state and hope that our competition won't do it as well, but why would they, those guys already know what we know and expect to win. Why fuck with a good thing?"

46. Close And Tight

Oregon has seven electoral votes. Polls showed it with an extremely close race but eventually going to Dyl's opponent, and a Direct Recording Electronic or DRE system of counting, in other words computers only tabulated by a supposedly protected process that couldn't, supposedly again, be hacked. Shifting a few votes one way or the other, or maybe adjusting the totals would make Dyl the winner and put him over the threshold to win the Electoral College.

The man they chose, eighteen years old and tall, thin as a rail, and white as a cleaned sheet, was perfect for the job. According to those in the know, he could hack his own brain if he knew of a harmless way inside it, but was otherwise so dumb he hadn't passed his English course in high school. He'd be making a five-figure salary when he graduated with only 'up' in front of him. He'd also likely starve to death by forgetting to eat long before then.

Tom told the kid this was an experiment only but that he should keep it secret or he might get caught and go to prison for a long time. Tom showed him his one-buck tin FBI fake badge to seal the deal and for a hundred bucks had his hacker.

With the networks clamoring for data as quickly as deliverable the night of the election, Tom and the kid decided that doing the dirty deed under the time constraints between closing time and sending was too stressful and thus Dyl, who's name was never mentioned, would have to call for a recount during which time their man could make the hack. This would give Dylan's opponent the opportunity to consider why Dyl hadn't capitulated, and within a day or so the whole election would shift to the Electoral College and things would get written in stone in December by anyone's count.

Dyl loved the whole thing. Tom hated it though it was his own idea. But it was what it was and it would achieve the desired result. The only question remaining was how the kid could break into a system completely cut off from the Internet, email, or have any relationship with the outside world. But the kid wasn't bothered by this apparently impossible barrier, so neither were Tom and Dyl, at least outwardly.

Why no one had thought of this possibility before haunted Tom. So simple, elegant, obvious, and non-transparent, someone must have figured it out before this. But apparently they hadn't. Or maybe they had and not gotten caught. We've might of had many Presidents in recent years who had not really won their elections.

Dylan was too busy appearing with his wife and kids to let any of this bother him. He wanted to win straight out, after all, not by getting down and dirty with the rest of the riff-raff. But time marched on and the last few days of what had been a near lifetime of wishing, hoping, working, fighting, talking, studying, and so on, was fast coming to an end. Why ordinary people would spend two years of their lives at this business only to find themselves locked in twenty or more major decisions per day any one of which could change the world for the worse in a split second was insane, and inane, truth be known. But for Dyl it meant everything. A rich bounty to be achieved. Power. Love. Money. All rolled in one magnificent step into the history books.

"Any last minute things left to do?" Dyl asked Tom before Election Day.

"Think we've covered it, Dyl."

"Any chance our little deceit could be discovered?"

"Always a chance. But not much of one."

"I'm ready to lose and recount my way into the history books?"

"Appears that way."

"Be my Chief of Staff, Tom?"

"Why not? That way you can keep an eye on me. Make sure I don't spill the beans."

Unbeknownst to Dyl and Tom, across town the major players in Dylan's party had not given up hope they could knock Dyl off if he happened to win. They knew the polls well and that he'd probably lose. Of course, they had no idea of Dyl's and Tom's plans to derail that loss. But taking no chances anyway, they'd talked the previous losing candidate for the highest office into a last minute write-in campaign that would take away votes for Dylan and make it truly impossible for him to succeed. Their write-in candidate wouldn't win either, but since he'd already lost once in the past, who the hell cared?

So the night before Election Day, every channel on America's television sets broadcast ad after ad for the voters to write in Chester Thomas as their choice for President. Unfortunately, their plan to remain anonymous as the funders of these ads created a rumor that it was Dyl's opponent who'd paid for the air time and thus, if anything, reduced the number of votes for the man they wanted to win rather than increase them.

This manifest mistake on their part left Tom and Dyl confused. Someone with a great deal of money—maybe twenty or so million dollars—had made a last ditch attempt to help his victory. Life for the Frye campaign had yet found another twist, this time, though, not of their own making.

47. The Day

When Election Day arrived, and no more chances to affect the voting remained, the world waited on pins and needles to see which of the two unacceptable candidates would win. The world would either face a carnival barker who'd huff and puff but never blow your house down, or a non-committal wienie who'd shy away from the Easter bunny.

As the day passed and no one heard a word from either candidate—a grace that most forgot immediately, the angst grew deep and intense. A special election this, for no one really knew their futures any longer, but a nuclear disaster certainly the best and worst simultaneously.

With so much to lose either way it went, nobody was shocked when several cities had riots break out, no doubt in frustration and desperation, most hoping that both candidates had joined the fray and been brutally murdered so that one or the other vice Presidential candidates could take over.

Such was not the case, though, for aside from litigations resulting from bumps and bruises, the frustration and disgust causing these outbursts provided nothing but a preview of the sideshows that were soon to follow and continue for the next four years.

"Any news?" Dyl asked Tom.

"Too close to call, Dyl."

"When do we ask for the recount?"

"You've got to lose first. No reason to ask for a recount if you win."

"You give me a chance to win?"

"Not much of one, no, but there's always a chance, Dyl. I've heard of stranger things happening."

"Like what?"

"Like a sand dab mating with an ostrich."

"What?"

"Had a baby as well."

"What kind of baby?"

"A sandwich, Dyl. C'mon, you're taking this too seriously."

"Seriously? I've only spent half my life at this, Tom. Half my life. You want serious? I'll give you serious!"

"Shut the fuck up, Dylan. You wouldn't know serious from the crack in your butt."

On and on it went, throughout the day and into the wee hours of the next as the votes kept slowly coming in and the leads changing hands every fifteen minutes. So close the call that no network, cable of otherwise, dared make a prediction.

Before dawn the day after the elections were held, one network and one only, took the leap and declared Dyl's opponent the loser of the popular vote but the winner of the more important electoral votes and the next President of the United States of America. With Oregon, both Tom and Dyl noticed, so close in votes that it would be nuts for Dylan not to call for a recount even with the ballots entered into and counted entirely by electrical and digital means.

No chance for a mistake if the technology worked as it should. Of course, since technology depended on humans to work perfectly and no one depended on humans for much of anything, Dyl's immediate claim for a recount met with an immediate positive response.

48. Recount

When the recount became known to the populace as a whole, Dyl suddenly, after he'd made sure the hacking plan was being carried out, received a flood of requests for an interview. He had nothing to lose. No one had a chance to vote again, and if their dirty little plan worked he'd win no matter what. So Dyl acquiesced to as many requests as he could.

"What do you expect the recount to prove, Mister Frye?"

"I have to say that lots of people have been asking this question. Lots of people, thousands, in fact. Many thousands. Tens of thousands."

Dyl had obviously unleashed one of his alternate personalities at this point but, again, what the hell?

"No really. A winner wins only if the tally proves it, right? You know what I mean? Many people want to know the count whether it's right or not. Not me. I want it right and that vote in Oregon is very close. *Very* close. A couple votes and the result of the electors would be very different."

"Do you suspect or have any reason to suspect that the computers made a mistake."

"Computers make mistakes. You know that. I know that. Everyone knows that. It's a nice question you ask. A very nice question. But you could have answered it yourself. Mistakes are possible. A vote supposedly goes one-way but turns out it goes the other way. It wouldn't be fair to the voters to cast their ballots to not get it perfectly right. Look, you wouldn't feel right about this either, would you? No, of course not. I love your questions by the way. You ask them the right way. No, you really do. The right way. You're probably my favorite interviewer. No, really. Really you are. I'm glad we're having this chance to talk. I love it. No, I really do. What else?"

"Will you be challenging any other state's vote in the election?"

"Another good question. We love you. We really do. So the answer is, I don't know. No other state had that close a result. I mean we're talking a couple of votes here. Look, that's too close to call. You know that and I know that. So we're going to take the high road. The high road. Look, we have these numbers and we add them together. Thousands of numbers. Hundreds of thousands. Maybe millions of them. It can't be that we get every one of them right, can it? No. I'm sure you agree with that. Hell, everyone agrees with that. It's the American way. The American way. The man who wins this election's going to be in charge of most everything. Right? Am I right? Yes, I'm right. He will have his paws on that famous red phone. The one that can start the big war to end all wars. No, I'm right and you know it. Right there, in his sleep almost, maybe, he'll hold our lives in his hand. One hand, nuclear war, the other hand us. BOOM, he claps his hands together and up we go in smoke. Precisely like that. BOOM! We have to be sure, you see. Good question. A very good question. Your audience loves that question and so do I. My answer? Well that was good as well. I give good answers. No, I really do. The best answers, really, if you must know."

"So, you're saying that you believe the current President elect, the one who currently has both the popular vote and the electoral vote until announced otherwise, would not be a person we could trust with the decision whether or not to use or not use nukes in a situation like that?"

"I'm saying that if he's President after the recount, then he's my President, too. That's what I'm saying. He's my President, too. You know that as well as me. Listen, I run hotels and casinos and make the best deals in the world. Millions of people, tens of millions of people sleep, gamble, and eat there at these hotels. You know that and I know that. People trust me. They should trust me. Trust is very important. If I ultimately win, you can trust me. I don't know whether you can trust him or not. Especially with that red phone. Pick that thing up and you're asking for it. I mean you're *really* asking for it. No, I mean it. I really do. You're asking for it. We're facing big stakes in this election. For the next four to eight years, big stakes I tell you. Listen, let's not get into a war that no one can win. I won't do that. I don't know if this other guy will or not. I certainly hope not and you do as well. Your readers do as well. Instead we need to rebuild our infrastructure, I tell you. Infrastructure. That's the important word here. Not have our bridges fall down with people dying. Hundreds of people. Maybe thousands or millions. Listen, I know this because I've driven our roads. Potholes? Everywhere. Deep ones. Our roads are falling apart. We need to fill those potholes up and keep us safe. Isn't that a better thing to be doing than starting a World War? I think so. I really do. So do you, I'm sure. Right?"

"Right. On a different topic, what do you think about a woman's right to abortion?"

"Easy. I'm pro-life."

"But what about rape and if the baby won't likely live if born?"

"Those are tough questions. They should prosecute the rapist and she should have the baby."

"That simple?"

"Sure."

"So you're against abortion in every case."

"I am."

"What if the mother's going to die if she has the baby?"

"Good question. There are obviously extenuating circumstances that have to be taken into account."

"So in that case you'd abort the baby."

"Depends."

"On what?"

"How sure the doctors were about it."

"About what?"

"About whether the mother would die or not."

"Okay, what if they were ninety percent sure."

"That's a lot. Listen, I won't kid you here, you're asking tough questions that only God can answer."

"So you don't know?"

"On what percentage this or that should happen? No, I don't. No one knows that. Only God."

"So you'd ask him if the matter were left up to you."

"What the hell you talkin' about. Why would it be left up to me? I'm not the rapist."

"No, you'd be the President and maybe have to make the decision."

"I'd follow the law."

"What is the law?"

"No abortions."

"Okay the mother dies and the baby lives. If that's the law, I'd uphold it."

"But laws can be changed. Would you change this law or recommend that the Supreme Court or Congress change it? Would you sign such a law if it were placed in front of you?"

"What law exactly is that?"

"The law we've been discussing."

"We've been discussing things in general not exact specifics. Listen, these things are complicated. You know that, I know that."

"What if a woman went against that law and got an abortion. What should happen?"

"Whatever the law says."

"Say the law says you have to arrest her."

"Arrest her."

"Is that your answer?"

"It is if that was the law. We have to follow the law. You know that. Listen. No, I mean it. We're off the deep end here. You realize that? We're way the hell and gone from reality here."

"But you would still arrest the woman not the doctor."

"What doctor?"

"The one performing the abortion."

"Whatever the law says."

"Would you try to change that law if that's what it said?"

"I'd give it a lot of thought before I did anything. Thinking is very important when you're the President, let me tell you. Right? Am I right?"

"You're right."

Tom listened to these interviews on radio, grimaced, and wondered why he considered the notion that Dylan would do a better job than the man currently in the winner's place. No contest. The weaker man would do better. Unfortunately, Tom had already put the hacker plan in motion and there was no way to put an end to it. No way.

So he hoped and prayed that the hacker would fail or get caught in the act and not inform on who had put him up to it.

49. Recount Deux

When the recount had concluded, Dyl's opponent still lost the popular vote but Dyl was declared the winner of the more important electoral vote and it took barely an hour before the press reported that Dylan's opponent had declared another miscount in Oregon and demanded a second recount to be sure.

Tom and Dyl should have considered this happening, but hadn't. They immediately checked with their eighteen-year-old hacker for what this second recount might reveal about their evil doings. The kid had no idea whether he'd left a digital trail behind. He knew they couldn't trace it to him and thus to Tom, but didn't have the slightest idea whether they would find evidence of the hack itself or not.

A day passed, and another, and the voters waited with baited breath for the outcome of the election. The whole process to them, from its beginning to it's not ending so far at least, had been bizarre at best. Of course, they pinned that bizarreness on Dylan who had, from the onset, acted like a circus ringmaster, whipping things into action while not knowing what would result as a consequence.

Dyl and Tom talked it over.

"You're now the President Elect," Tom said.

"I am," Dyl answered.

"But tomorrow you may be the loser and your name will be dust."

"True."

"So what do we do about that?"

"That's the question."

"What can we do about it?"

"Ask for another recount if I lose this time?"

"I doubt they'd do that without figuring that someone, you most likely, was fooling around by hacking the system somehow."

"Right. So If I lose this time, I'm out?"

"Guess that's what I'm saying."

"What about us getting the kid to do another hack?"

"The feds are working on the recount."

"Yeah. Guess so."

"I don't know for sure if they wouldn't catch him red handed."

"Anyway, can you make sure about that?"

"Could call him and ask."

"Be a good idea."

"I will. Right now?"

"Can't think of a better time."

"Okay. I'll call you when I find out."

"Thanks."

When the phone rang, Dylan was on it like a hawk on a titmouse.

"Dyl?"

"Well?"

"He doesn't know. Could get caught. Might not."

"The odds?"

"He says fifty-fifty."

"So if he gets caught, we get the blame and hope he doesn't spill the beans."

"Probably."

"If he doesn't get caught, there's still a fifty-fifty chance we'll lose."

"Why's that?"

"Changing it back may alert them to something happening, and since my opponent won on the initial count they might leave it that way and forget the recounts."

"Maybe."

"That makes it seventy-five to twenty-five that I'll lose. Don't like those odds."

"If those odds are right. Could be wrong. You're making a lot of assumptions there."

"I am."

"So?"

"So what?"

"What do we do?"

"I have no idea. Your call."

"My call? You're the man, Dyl. You're the man. It's your call."

"This is nuts, Tom. This is truly nuts. Let's call it when we get the results."

"That sounds good to me."

"Good to me as well."

The days passed yet again with no one the wiser for it. The feds wanted to get it right this time and had hired an independent firm to do a thorough job on the digital files involved to see how the glitches could have occurred. No one knew how long the process would take. Or at least no one was taking a guess over how long.

When the results were finally announced, some sighed sighs of relief, others cried, and still others celebrated. The way it was when elections became this discombobulated.

50-1. Someone Upstairs

Despite winning the popular vote by over twenty thousand ballots, Dylan Frye lost the Electoral College by seven votes after two recounts. He and Tom regretted not going for a third recount, but clearly someone upstairs in a Federal Building somewhere had caught them in the act and keeping the charade going wouldn't work a second time around.

Katrina, his kids, and Dyl's dog Gloria felt demolished given the years that he and they had spent attempting to save the country from a disaster that would certainly occur with this new shamelessly vacant coward in charge. They were wrong, of course, since the one thing this coward knew was that he *was* a coward who listened to those who advised him, not going off half-cocked to solve problems he knew nothing about. In short, he spent most of his time getting advice and acting when his staff had reached consensus, something that Dylan would never have done. Could never have done.

Dyl returned to his real estate firm, paid the now jobless vice President back with interest on his loan, and once again used his shameless tactics and bravura to put his life back together again. Of course, the one thing that Dyl could never do is take defeat sitting down, and thus within a month or two had already begun his second campaign for President of the United States of America.

Tom had already hit the trail and so Dylan hired a new Chief of Staff for his nascent campaign and worked on other more shameless ways to demean personalities in his presentations, thus making him seem incredibly strong and fearless. Unfortunately, he'd never apparently gotten the notion that knowing what he was talking about had anything to do with the American electorate. He'd come within a few votes of making it the last time. On this occasion, he'd stretch himself a bit further and take the job away from the incumbent.

He divorced his wife and once again avowed his love for his dog Gloria before marrying for a fourth time, this woman a fake-breasted porn star who had ways of making him happy that he'd never given thought to before. He traveled the world to see what he'd missed the first time, bragged about his billionaire lifestyle to those who could stand to listen to him, and attempted to build entire cities in his image but eventually failed.

Throughout this, Dylan never lost sight of love, power, and money, though he learned along the way someplace that his true love, the one that his use of the word 'love' embraced, was the one he saw in the mirror every day. Never apologizing to anyone, loving those who loved him, getting even with those who didn't, and trying desperately to take everything he'd supposedly earned with him when he died.

Whether be became President or not on his next venture though the campaign circuit I leave to you, the reader. I've left enough hints lying around as loose ends here to sagely make your own decision.

Whatever happened to Dyl, though, and whatever opinion you may have of him as you've read these lines, know that without him, the world might be a better place, but it would as well be a much duller one.

50-2. Winner Take All

Dyl and Tom, against both their better judgments, decided to go for a third recount and, for a couple of days felt safe from discovery of their second attempt at hacking the ballots. Then, without warning, their best attempts and the attempts of their hacker went for naught as those in charge announced that tampering had been found and, while no one could find out who'd done it, the multiple recounts were finished. Dylan had lost the race by virtue of having less than fifty percent of the electorates and thus his opponent had secured the next four years as President of the United States.

Everyone involved in the campaign mourned the loss but mourning, as often as it achieves some measure of making the mourners feel at least a little better, didn't, and everyone went their separate ways. Except those, of course, that worked for one of Dylan's still non-bankrupted companies.

It turned out that the new President did indeed prove a disaster, with him having a ten percent approval rating before the first month of his tenure had transpired. Dyl, of course, wanted someone to interview him so he could say he told you so, but his views on such matters were of no interest to those assigning interviews. He was a loser, after all. The economy went haywire with the stock market achieving lows so low that no one alive had seen them so low in their lifetimes.

The one good thing from this, though, turned out to be a sudden lack of wars. As the U. S. went, so went the world, and no country or terror group could afford to declare war on any other and thus, broke and with poverty reaching new highs in poverty stricken countries the world over, death by battle also sunk to new lows.

Dyl, who could have returned himself to one of the richest of the rich in two or three years, found himself trying to sell off his self-named towers to no one. Seems that the one percent of the country no longer had that honor. They, it turned out, proved as vulnerable as anyone else in this new and crumbling mess and Dyl found himself holding great riches in real estate that really had no value whatsoever.

Eventually K divorced him and took the kids, and his dog Gloria, tired of not getting fed, and vanished one night into the moors never to be seen again.

As we watch Dyl attempting to get his ten-year-old PC to function without success, we see him screaming and pounding on his desk in disgust at what might have been were it not for such things as electoral colleges and voters who couldn't see their way out of wet paper bags.

Of course, none of this would have happened if he hadn't accepted those interviews that had reduced his chances or been caught trying to rig the system. Life had played a dirty trick on him and he'd have to live with it. Forever. Banging on his desk for his computer to magically heel itself would never happen in a million years.

50-3. Who's In Charge

Believe it or not, the appropriate governmental agency assigned to recount votes in a particular state to help determine it's electoral count, did not discover the kid's truly professional hack, and thus, to the great surprise of Tom, Dyl, and the kid himself, Dylan Frye won the election in terms of both the popular vote and the rigged electoral count and became the fortieth something President of the United States of America.

President Frye went immediately into overdrive and took his Congress—yes the Congress that both Senate and representatives had gone over to his party—on a joy ride into his version of the perfect government, one of low overhead, high rent, and where half the country began a descent into the lowest class. Charles Dickens would have been disgusted with what Dylan accomplished in his first year. America had become a perfect monarchy with everything that caste systems were enjoyed by the upper class and despised by the lower classes.

The trickle down theory upon which he'd based budgets and which Congress had passed with gusto, trickled up instead. The rich got richer, much richer, and the poor became homeless, living with the rats and other homeless people that survived the winters surrounding fires within metal barrels to keep warm, and whatever looked edible as food. Once again, gangs roamed the streets of the richest cities providing drive-by shootings and robberies willy-nilly. Life sucked, to put it bluntly, with only those at the top, the ones able to smile slightly at their humbled existence, reduced to having one less maid or lowering the salaries of their servants to minimum, wages to keep themselves from dropping from the elite to the semi-elite.

50-4. Pulling The Trigger

The kid, the one assigned a duty that he had to accomplish twice instead of once, did so with aplomb and Dylan Frye won the election with several electoral votes to spare. And a good time was had by all. The capitol lit up like a Christmas tree with only lights of white, and the party proved so extravagant as to nearly bankrupt the country, no less Dyl's real estate company.

Unfortunately, however, with but a few weeks of bad decisions in terms of the economy, a masked man, having taken heart that the country had to lay off several of their armed security guards, assassinated the newly elected President leaving the country entirely in the hands of the new vice President, a man named Wilkes Booth mentioned previously in these pages.

The shooter, as irony would have it, claimed he shot and killed the President for making himself richer off the hard-working backs of America's workers of which he claimed himself one, though he'd never held a job in his life. Of any kind. At least not a paying one given that he'd been raised and kept by one of the richest families in America, a family kept in financial good graces by his father's ownership of a fracking company notorious for tearing up countryside by the thousands of acres to release natural gas inside rocks.

VP Booth had been chosen for his milquetoast version of politics and his continuous clashes with Congress, though both were run by members of the same party as he, and them running over him faster than a revved-up race car. It turned out that the person who produced the phrase, "A camel is a horse created by a committee," was precisely right. You'd have thought that the famous Capitol Hill existed in the Middle East rather than in Washington, D. C. since the entire town seemed run over by such camels. Actually, the entire country with the exception of certain parts of Nevada and Utah, quickly developed the same problems.

It turned out that the Peter Principle also still worked. Workers rose to their highest level of incompetence and kept their tenure there for the rest of their lives.

50-5. Hard Knocks

After several more recounts, Dylan Frye eventually won the election and became President of the United States to his great surprise. Unfortunately for him, though, the stress of the long haul to become the President took a terrible toll on his health such that he became deathly ill for months before recovering, by which time his number two man, the vice President, had run the country into the sewer, both literally and figuratively. He invaded, much to everyone's surprise, every country that suggested they might be interested in war with anyone else, and the military ran itself ragged trying to keep up with their assignments.

Initially, the doctors thought that Dylan had been poisoned for two reasons. One, that they could find nothing wrong with him except a constant fever, a strange lisp he'd developed, his tendency to go off on tangents when speaking that made very little sense, and that he was losing weight. No sign of cancer or anything else that could be the cause. Second, he wasn't aware that he'd become President and that he was wasting away as his career as such was getting shot to shit. They seriously suspected that someone had been putting a slow acting and quickly disappearing deadly drug into his meals, maybe a cook or a server at the table, but nothing could be proved. Once that suspicion was checked, he got better.

Eventually, though, when speaking to him, they discovered that no matter the question they asked, he would reply with, "I have nothing against lesbians, gays, bisexuals, or transgender people." That's it. Word for word. Every time they asked him a question. For example, "What would you like for dinner tonight?" he'd answer with, "I have nothing against lesbians, gays, bisexuals, or transgender people."

Thus, most every day of his four-year term was handled by Wilkes Booth, the Vice President, who lost the reelection in the following term by a landslide that their own party joined in ensuring. Dylan, still in his more or less coma of LGBT recursions, spent the rest of his life in a psychiatric facility with him having gained the world record for election to the presidency with but only three days in office. Of course, while staying alive for the remaining years, months, weeks, days, and hours of his initial term.

Katrina, Dylan's kids, and his dog Gloria visited him on occasion to see if by some odd chance Dyl might come to his senses again, but it never happened. Apparently the man of two minds about things also had two lives, the former switching back and forth at will, and the latter switching only once late in life.

Dylan died never knowing about his record, his non-presidency, and his fortune which, due to his wife's spending habits, had dwindled to the point of non-existence before she died, leaving what little was available to their children and by that time their children's children.

But he would have been proud of the blinking versions of his last name that still appeared, at least for a few years following, on the sides and at the tops of his hotel/casinos in various large cities around the country and, of course, Las Vegas, Nevada.

A sneak Preview of
David Cope's bestselling novel
Dark Money.

1.

In the small town of Frostport on the Elk River in central West Virginia lived a junior reporter named Quinn Quartermain. His job involved covering the local sports scene that typically consisted of Frostport High School's football, basketball, and wrestling teams with occasional mentions of its baseball program that hadn't had a single winning season in its nearly hundred-year history. At nearly thirty years of age at this point, Quartermain could have wished for more, but in these hard times, a job was a job, and a job in one's chosen field held extra weight as far as he was concerned.

While Quinn had been born in Charleston, fifty-five miles to the west of Frostport, he'd been raised entirely in the smaller town and attended the local schools. So, working for Frostport's one newspaper— the Daily Call—was a natural for him. And he'd 'majored' in football in high school, and thus the assignment to sports was natural as well. Furthermore, beyond attempting to write the great American novel, Quinn spent much of his spare time fishing for trout in the local Elk River that fed into the Kanawha and Ohio rivers that eventually led to the great Mississippi. The Elk crossed some of the roughest terrain in eastern and central West Virginia, or so the brochures advertising its beauties attested. A geological marvel, it often channeled through subterranean networks of caves, dropped over many falls, and in extremely dry weather was known to flow completely underground in large sections where it could be heard but not seen, and with only dry sand where the water normally flowed. He loved the area and everything in it except the winters, with maybe fifty inches of snow yearly and daily highs in the mid-thirties.

Quinn had not gotten far with his novel over the years. A potboiler about a fictional family living off the river in the nineteenth century, he'd based the plot on an old legend about a mysterious man's story told to the Call and printed in the Local Lore section. Something about it caught Quinn's eye and gave him the notion that the details held a truly important American story worth telling. But he'd wrestled with describing the period he'd known nothing about, and was now stalling his obvious need to spend weeks in local libraries reading and researching the dialects, properties, and cultural artifacts of the times. Still, he enjoyed introducing himself to others as a novelist, and so he did.

He'd left home when he'd graduated high school, finding a flat above a garage nearer the center of town and the newspaper. He'd toyed with night school at the local junior college, but creative writing classes left him as clueless as the teachers, and he realized his only rationale for taking the courses was to meet women, and the ones he met were the ones he already knew. No sense paying for that, so he quit before he finished and dated on and off. But the ladies he chose had but one thing in mind, and his career came before marriage, especially before kids.

The days, weeks, months, and now years had passed, and Quinn Quartermain had lived up to his name. A true penny-pincher, with a three-day a week job at a hick newspaper, in a hick town, with a hick boss, and nowhere to go but more of the same. Not unhappy, mind you, but losing faith that he'd one day get to tackle a big story revealing some previously hidden crime, dirty laundry, or win a prize of some kind, if only a local one.

He'd begun with such high hopes with his own newspaper at age twelve. A weekly in which he collected stories from the neighborhood, ads from local businesses, and classifieds from those wanting someone to mow their lawns or shovel their snow and, using moveable type, set up his hand printer and made several copies at ten cents apiece, and he always sold out, at the time thinking his audience were fans only to discover later that they often lined their garbage cans with the results of his hard work.

This experience quickly drove him to spice up his columns with bits of gossip not so friendly to those who supplied the material. This drove up circulation, but it also drove down his ability to acquire stories. Once, when the thought he'd nailed a headline and associated column with a piece about an old man who lived nearby who'd apparently stolen someone's horse, the life of his Harbor Times ended. Circulation of one hundred at its peak, its fate disappeared down the tubes with a threat of litigation against his parents who, as one might imagine, were not so happy about Quinn's attempts to succeed in one tough business.

Prom night hit Quinn like a ton of bricks. First he lost his virginity to someone else's girl, a pity-date he guessed, for she was not the brightest nor prettiest of the girls there that night. She'd struck up a conversation with him outside the dance and before long had wrestled him to the outside grounds and one thing led to another. Even though Quinn had no doubt the date who'd brought her—a big, ugly and stupider brontosaurus-type with fossilized scars on his cheeks—wasn't actually jealous, the guy threw a lucky punch and as testosterone would have it, barreled into Quinn's midsection before Quinn had a chance to respond. They both then made the *Call*'s headlines the next morning, bloody photos. Luckily, however, the editor, Quinn's soon-to-be boss at the time, had a short memory for such things.

Thus, Quartermain's parents were not so unhappy when their son, at age eighteen, moved out and set up shop elsewhere. They'd put up with his childish newspaper, with worrying about him during the years he played football and would often return home bloodied and bruised from his offensive lineman position, with his lack of a steady girlfriend and similar lack of desire to get married, and with having no job of worth, and had had it. His sister, who apparently had everything Quinn didn't, received lots of kudos, and the two of them fought, bitterly at times, to the admonishment of both parents, sick of the feud between them that had grown over the years.

So, by the time Quinn Quartermain reached his eighteenth birthday, he'd apparently failed at most everything. Except, of course, his hiring on with the Daily Call for three days a week to pay the rent on his flat, a desolate, lonely, miserable, and nearly intolerable place that only fishing and occasionally his job made bearable.

Again, even though it might not seem so, Quinn loved Frostport. Even though it represented the whole of what he knew of the world having only twice visited the state capital where he'd been born, he found it a great place to live. And he did have friends besides women. Joe Matte, for example, a cohort on the football team during high school. Joe barely passed his courses and couldn't speak coherently no less write that way, but he and Quinn palled around together a lot of the time, though they were diametric opposites. Joe was a rather outspoken racist. Quinn, not. Joe drank a good deal and smoked weed. Again, Quinn not. But they spent a lot of time fishing together, and somehow minimalized their somewhat drastic differences.

After graduation, though, Joe joined the army and Quinn remained in Frostport. He missed Joe briefly, but later realized that the only good his friend had done him was to cement his own views more solidly. Joe wouldn't have appreciated that observation, but Quinn swore to himself it was true. They never argued about these differences, but thinking them over made Quinn realize the depth of Joe's ignorance and the truth of his own beliefs.

But Joe's departure made a hole in Quinn's off-day schedules allowing him to read, another difference between the two high school chums. Quinn loved Hemingway's *For Whom the Bell Tolls*, for instance. Joe had never heard of Hemingway, no less the book. *East of Eden* by Steinbeck was another favorite. In short, after he moved to his flat, Quinn noticed the number of books he'd bought, borrowed on extended loan from his parents, or found in the one used bookstore in Frostport had increased in number dramatically. He even had a rare edition of the history of the town in which he lived, a copy of the original. There he'd learned the origin of the name of the town—a melding of poet Robert Frost's last name and a bottle of port Frost apparently liked to drink occasionally—something Quinn never would have guessed on his own.

Frostport itself covered six city blocks of stores and businesses, all fronting Main Street and crowded together as if zoning had prohibited any outward growth. On one end of town, the Daily Call held reign. At the other, the city Hall and Police Department had their offices in a one-story plain building that, were it not for the signs, might have been considered housing for the homeless. As if holding their two sides of the street together, the two buildings—the Call and The Hall as townspeople referred to them—held sway in opposition to one another. The Junior College might have broken the clustering were it not positioned in an old apartment building one block over from Main. Thus, with the exception of the College, visitors driving through saw everything there was to see in

Frostport in one quick pass. Blink and you missed it, don't blink and you wouldn't.

The town barely fit in a small pocket of land through which the Elk flowed, with hills on each side behind the town's center. These hills mixed conifers and oaks in such a way that, when fall turned the leaves of the deciduous type into colorful visions, the forest made living in town a beautiful thing to behold. For two to three weeks then in the fall, Frostport grew in size to accommodate visitors, from instate and out, and the businesses there blossomed with new customers along with the vibrant mix of seasons.

Through his trials, tribulations, and scares from his reporting duties and living in such a town reminiscent more of New England than the mid-west, Quinn Quartermain retained his one true love, that of being a writer. Forget that he couldn't yet author the great American novel. Forget that he hadn't attracted a member of the fair sex for more than one date. Forget that he hadn't caught the big fish in the Elk or gotten a full-time job. He was only thirty and getting the experience he needed to eventually make the big time. No longer a naïve young reporter, but still having the 'junior' attached to his job title, he would eventually come into his own. He was sure of it.